Jilly's ability to see way beyond your immediate situation provides all those that work with her and read her extraordinary book with an incredible opportunity to move way beyond the limitations of whatever is happening and see, feel and experience energetic shifts and ultimately... freedom!

She works outside the mind by helping you open into your own truth: a deep body remembering, a soul remembering of unconditional love, where Jilly reminds us that there is always hope and that anything can change in an instant. I've had many profound experiences of that while working with her.

I have never known anyone else that works in this way and Jilly's dedication to her own growth and then assisting others to remember who they truly are on an energetic, heart and soul level, is unparalleled. That's what makes her and her work so unique and effective.

Trish Warner – Midwife/Energy Healer – Sydney

Being conditioned by business I thought I was doing everything 'right' – being successful, following the rules, only to realize I was never meant to live that way. And while 'self-love' is something we hear often, what does it really mean? I feel Jilly walks us through each chapter with different perspectives so we can experience what it is for ourselves.

This is not a motivational book or about following someone else's path, it offers a practical, deeply relatable way to develop your own awareness through letting go of old beliefs and habits and finally coming home to your authentic self.

Kathy Vergotis – Successful Multi-Business Owner – Sydney/Adelaide

Jilly is a very gifted professional. Her down to earth nature and cut to the chase ability to create a safe space to help release trauma is amazing. She understands the fragility of our humanness and works to open new pathways for fresh possibilities to emerge – she's a gift!

Clint Smith – Personal/Professional Client – Queensland

The group sessions Jilly has facilitated for our community have been powerful and we're so grateful for her generosity to guide us. She consistently tunes into the precise place where each woman feels stuck, regardless of their challenge or trigger. Each time she creates a space that is both safe and expansive on a personal and collective level. These sessions allow them to witness the pain without becoming trapped in their story, resistance, or trauma responses, enabling them to move toward genuine empowerment.

Monthly Groupwork Zoom Sessions – Sydney Women's Community

Working with Jilly has been deeply transformative. Her work brings an energetic focus that feels both grounding and expansive, allowing me to stretch into new levels of growth while feeling safe and supported.

Through our time together, I have activated a stronger sense of inner leadership and agency in both my life and purpose-driven work. Jilly helped me shift from survival-based patterns into clarity, truth, and trust in my own inner knowing and from that place I now stand stable as a leader in so many ways.

She has supported me in all my roles: as a new leader, mentor, mother, friend, and creative, while compassionately reflecting the deeper truth that was there all along. After years of navigating trauma and endless self-improvement, our work together helped me access a profound sense of safety and alignment within myself. I'm so honored and grateful to have her as a guide on this journey!

Danielle – Executive Leadership Mentoring – Sydney

Working with Jilly has given me a higher awareness of my life, which is one of the most amazing things I could gain. With every passing session I became closer to understanding who my true self was, especially as we've navigated through so many different obstacles that life has thrown at me. As someone who used to struggle with identity issues, Jilly has empowered me and equipped me with the tools to enjoy life again and be aligned with my truth, emotionally, physically and spiritually. If you are ready to challenge your mind, heal your wounds and open your heart, Jilly is the best way to tackle all three!

M.J. – Personal Client – Sydney

When I read Jilly's book I found it confronting at times as it made me tune in and be honest about where I really was in my life. I needed to go beyond what I knew, to genuinely have a look at my thoughts, beliefs and behaviors. I must admit as I started to unravel, I experienced many 'light bulb moments' where I shed a few tears, and then I finally got it! It was as if I woke up from a long sleep. Thank you Jilly, I've known you for many years and I wish you all the success you so truly deserve.

Kerry E – Business Women – Western Australia

I have known and worked with Jilly Gabrielson for a number of years and would highly recommend her. When I owned a large business with many staff, my management team worked with Jilly to help them emotionally, mentally and physically run a successful business that focused on providing genuine care for staff and customers, as well as being financially viable.

Debi Kearney – Business Women – Queensland

Working with Jilly is a truly uplifting experience. Her understanding and ability to connect practically and emotionally was deeply insightful.

Jilly's unique ability to identify growth steps in her sessions made a real difference to how I managed and more recently, she has helped me see personal matters with fresh eyes.

Anne Poole, MHRM – Holistic Career Coach and Author

Jilly creates a space that is both safe and expansive, a place where you can question, reflect, and ultimately step more fully into who you are meant to be.

What I appreciated most was her grounded wisdom. Nothing felt forced or prescriptive. Instead, she helped illuminate pathways that allowed me to reconnect with my own intuition and sense of direction. That process brought a deep sense of freedom, the kind that comes when you realise you are far more capable and empowered than you once believed.

The impact of that work continues to ripple through my life. I feel lighter, clearer, and far more open to the opportunities and experiences life presents. Working with Jilly didn't just change my perspective, it expanded my world and reminded me that we are all capable of far more than we often allow ourselves to imagine.

Tamara de Lange – Former Operations and HR Manager Kunara Group

I've known Jilly for a long time as an insider and outsider of her life's journey. I have seen and experienced the significant life transformation that she has embarked upon, and the never-ending determination she displays to understand herself, others and the bigger picture.

I have witnessed her skilful work with my business teams and executive mentoring and have been grateful for the insightful and different perspectives shared to help team cohesion.

Jilly's views on life and love have never been those of a conformist. She challenges the norms and seeks the truth in her own, others and life itself. At times I have been challenged by this however she has always found a way through and we remain connected to this day.

When I read her book I found in opened greater understanding of things previously not accessible to me. It has wisdom, purpose and great tools. It lets you explore the bigger picture of your life and reflect on both the now and the choices we have moving forward, it is a really worthwhile read!

JW – International Businessman CEO

'If you want to find the secrets of the Universe,
think in terms of energy, frequency and vibration.'
–Nikola Tesla

ENERGY MATTERS!

9 Transformational Gateways to Greater **FREEDOM, TRUTH** and **LOVE**

JILLY GABRIELSON

Published in Australia by
Bright Spark Health
jilly@brightsparkhealth.com.au
www.brightsparkhealth.com.au

First published in Australia 2026
Copyright © Jilly Gabrielson 2026

National Library of Australia Cataloguing in Publication entry

 A catalogue record for this book is available from the National Library of Australia

ISBN 978-1-7645496-0-8 (paperback)
ISBN 978-1-7645496-1-5 (hardback)
ISBN 978-1-7645496-2-2 (epub)

Cover design by Luigi99 on 99designs
Design and typeset by Sophie White Design
Printed by Ingram Spark

Foreword

When my mum asked me to write the foreword to her book my immediate response was, "Wouldn't you prefer someone well-known to do it? You've worked with, business leaders, politicians and celebrities, so why me?"

She responded "Well, yes, I've met many people at different stages of my life but for more than the last half of it, you've been the one constant. You're the one who's probably most qualified to talk about the transformation I've experienced from being a first-time mother to the woman I am today."

I sat on that for a bit and thought about my thirty six years of moments I've had with Mum and all the events we'd gone through in her life, early memories of school pick-ups and lunches flooded my mind. Times she wasn't just my mum, but also my confidant, counselor, and friend. Through hardships at school, and truth be told, some even harder moments in my life. Through it all, the most obvious point is that there's nothing like a mother's love.

However, this isn't a parenting book, it's a story about transformation, a story about a woman who has constantly evolved throughout her life. It's a journey of sometimes playing a different character and at times being trapped inside somebody else's body, not knowing her purpose, navigating through challenges to finally connect with her true self.

It's not a manual telling people how to live their lives, or how they should think or feel, because to me, one size doesn't fit all. That is probably one of the best lessons that my mum taught me: there is no playbook for life. There isn't a path that you just do or a set course that defines us. It's a series of moments living in the present that you try to bring together into the rich tapestry that is our life. We romanticize the past and often fear the future, yet how we act and live in the present is one of the only things we can control.

Jilly might not be everyone's cup of tea, hell, I've probably been her biggest skeptic for most of my life. Nor will every message resonate with every reader, but I've always found an element of truth in what she says. I have appreciated the tools she provided, the frameworks that guided my decisions, and never felt pressure to act in a certain way or do a certain thing. So I hope you enjoy this book, and experience it in many different ways. Perhaps pick it up and put it down as needed. Save it for your next big decision, or simply when you want to reflect on the bigger picture.

Fortunately, I don't have to buy this book to learn the wisdom contained within. However, for those of you who are about to meet Jilly for the first time, all I can say is, you're in for a real experience. As she would say to me in this moment – don't focus endlessly on the words in front of you and analyze their every possible meaning, just feel what the message is sharing and what that stirs in you.

It's time to let the magic happen!

– Jack Walker

Preface

Energy Matters!

The perspectives in this book may feel very different from the way most of us have been taught to live. What I share here is not presented as absolute truth, more an insight, experience, and a deeper remembering. My hope is that these words open gateways for you to reflect upon your own life choices, and uncover a resonance that is already within.

This book explores change, not as something imposed from outside, but as an inner movement, gently guided by the invisible expansion of our soul's resonance. At its heart, a reminder that we each hold a unique note, a universal harmonic of unconditional love and when we live in alignment with our tune, the denser, heavier energies of the material world can dissolve and give space for greater truths to be revealed.

The reality we see around us today is often dominated by control, polarity, and division. Judgments of right/wrong, good/bad, black/white labels are given to shape how people are considered and treated. This duality keeps victimhood alive, convincing us that life happens *to us*, rather than *through us*.

We acknowledge the suffering and horrors in the world, however, real change begins in an unexpected place; within! Transformation unfolds when we stop blaming others for our circumstances and instead claim our sovereignty, our freedom to respond, to create, and to make different choices.

This book does not deny the weight of the world. Instead, it invites you to travel through nine transformational gateways to help you remember something that may have been forgotten. I do not profess to have the answers, only to share a path I have walked, with all its vulnerability, questions, and discoveries laid bare.

The underlying context is, that at some point before birth, each of us said "yes" to our mission! We chose to be here, now, in this body, with these humans, in this environment, to bring our unique vibration into physical form. We are here to help ourselves and humanity remember: we came from love, we are love and we return to love.

Contents

Foreword — 7

Preface – Energy Matters! — 9

Transformational Gateway Structure — 14

Introduction — 16

Our Adventure Begins — 18

Energy Matters! — 21

Beyond the Illusion Story – The Sound Of Home — 23

The Leap — 25

New Beginnings — 26

Beyond the Illusion — 27

First Remembering Opens! — 28

Where Did It All Start? — 31

Self-Help Through the Decades — 33

A Snapshot of Self-Help/Spiritual Evolution — 35

Body and Healing — 36

Gateway One **Remembering** — 43
The Truth of Human Beings
The Lost Compass — 45
World of Duality — 48
How do I gain the most from each gateway exercise? — 52
Remembering Exercises — 53

Gateway Two **The Driver's Seat** — 59
Realizing We Have Been Passengers In Life
Head in the Sand — 63
Driven By Fear — 66
Can a Bed Make the Difference? — 68
Driver's Seat Exercises — 70

Gateway Three **Natural Connection** — 75
Symbiosis Of All Living Things
Mountain Awakening — 78
Cost of Separation — 80
Abundance Web — 82
Natural Connection Exercises — 84

Gateway Four	**Untrue Belief Systems**	**89**
	Dissolving Old Restrictive Patterns	
	The Invisible	95
	Vulnerability Dissolves Barriers	97
	Buried Treasure Of You!	100
	Changing Restrictive Beliefs	102
	Untrue Belief Systems Exercises	102

Gateway Five	**Inner Senses**	**105**
	Listening to the Body's Wisdom	
	Wake Up Body	108
	Beingness	111
	The River – Ability to Go With the Flow	114
	Inner Senses Exercises	116
	Breathwork – Source of Life	*117*
	Movement – Body Reset	*117*
	Journaling	*119*
	Sleep	*119*
	Nature Walking	*120*
	Fuel & Nourishment	*120*
	Environmental Energetics	*121*
	Emotional Healing Therapies	*121*
	Body-Based Healing	*122*
	Spiritual Connection Practices	*123*

Gateway Six	**Communication**	**125**
	Effective Exchange Changes Everything	
	The Unheard Communication	129
	Feeling Communication	133
	What Lies Below the Surface?	135
	Communication Exercises	138

Gateway Seven	**Challenges**	**145**
	Pathways Through Barriers	
	On My Own	149
	Challenge is Breakthrough Point	152
	Intellectual Awareness Changes Nothing	153
	Challenges Exercises	155

Gateway Eight	**Creativity**	**161**
	The Flow of Conscious Expression	
	Pig in Mud	164
	Love Creation – A personal story for you!	168
	Creativity Exercises	171
Gateway Nine	**Restoration of Original Love**	**175**
	Key to Finding the Unconditional Within	
	Not What It Seems	179
	Child Beingness	180
	Love of The Father	183
	Restoration of Original Love Exercises	184
Summary	**The Veil Lifts**	**189**
	Freedom, Truth and Love is Revealed	
	How Can We Do This?	191
Thank You!		192
Big Picture Summary		193
Support		214
Contact		215
About The Author		216
Acknowledgments		217

Transformational Gateway Structure

Stepping through each energy gateway, you will discover:

1. **Remembering** – The Truth of Human Beings

2. **Driver's Seat** – Realizing We Have Been Victims to Life

3. **Natural Connection** – Symbiosis of All Living Things

4. **Untrue Belief Systems** – Dissolving Old Restrictive Patterns

5. **Internal Senses** – Listening to the Body's Wisdom

6. **Communication** – Effective Exchange Changes Everything

7. **Challenges** – Pathways Through Barriers

8. **Creativity** – The Flow of Conscious Expression

9. **Restoration of Orginal Love** – Key to Finding the Unconditional Within

Each energy gateway is structured to include:

* A **concept** that expands awareness

* A **bigger picture** view to connect personal with universal

* A **personal story** from the author's own experience

* A **scientific quote** to establish common viewpoints

* A **professional lens** drawing on decades of therapeutic and holistic expertise

* A **client story** offering real-world transformation

* **Exercises and tools** to support the reader's own awakening

* **Reflections and diagrams** to bring clarity and resonance

Introduction

I was always fascinated by life and what it was *really* about, beyond the roles we play, the stories we tell, and the identities we cling to. I was drawn to feelings, emotions, invisible forces that seem to shape who we are, who we become and what we do with that.

While working in the corporate world, I found myself repeatedly drawn to personal development courses. At the time, I didn't fully understand why. Looking back, I can see I was searching for balance, some reassurance that there was more to us than performance, productivity, and survival. I was looking for a deeper cause for our existence.

On one of those workshops, in a moment I could never have planned, my whole life took a 180 degree turn!

While sitting with a group of people, I started to observe myself. My posture was tight and upright as if I was in a boardroom with everything under control, but inside was the exact opposite. I was in utter turmoil! My thoughts were running rampant, saying, "Jilly, you've got everything: a kind husband, child, friends, career, homes, cars, boat... your life's perfect!" Yet at that moment, none of that mattered. It seemed as though everything had been stripped away leaving me naked and fearful the group would see right through me.

I felt deeply flawed, broken and a failure, a 'me' I'd never known, let alone shown to the world!

It was my turn to speak and I couldn't, the words wouldn't come out. Then one person, in a most kind and loving gesture, started to share how they felt about me, then another, then another and another, to the point I couldn't receive any more loving acknowledgments as my heart felt like it would explode!

It was then I sensed an uncontrollable feeling increasing and it began to rise.

It felt like a wave, emotional, physical, spiritual, undeniable, and then it spoke to me...

"Are you willing to let go?"

I saw this internal image where I was standing on the edge of a cliff, certain death looming below if I jumped, yet in that moment, without hesitation, I said "yes" and let go!

My body buckled forward and all I could see was radiant white light, as if my heart had exploded and a reality shift had taken place. That single moment altered the trajectory of my life forever.

Had I have known the choices I would be faced with, involving my identities, beliefs, control and attachments, I doubt I would have said "yes". Maybe that's why there is a sense of going backwards through life as we don't know what's ahead of us until we do!

That "yes" moved me from the safety and security of the known into the discomfort and risk of the unknown. It began the heartbreaking, honest, and joyful unraveling of the stories and emotions I had constructed to feel safe, accepted, and valued by the world.

I've wondered subsequently if life is predestined, or do we all have numerous choice points where we are asked "Are you ready to let go or not?" and life reflects our choice!

Our Adventure Begins

How do we remember our note, our original tune, the one we infinitely play in the Universal Orchestra of life? Even with eight billion people on the planet your note is uniquely yours, and you came here to play it. NOW is the time to start playing!

I invite you to follow that call to the vast and vibrant truth already alive *within*. Through this thread, we'll **dissolve patterns of fear, fragmentation and forgetting**, that have kept us disconnected from our original note.

Each of the nine gateways guides us through portals of transformation. It's an adventure of awakening designed to be **walked and felt**, as it is read, **blending personal stories, client breakthroughs, timeless spiritual concepts, practical tools, and heartfelt insights.** Together, these elements illuminate the **parts of ourselves we've lost, neglected, or denied,** and guide us gently **home to our core tune.**

All the gateways work independently but can also be followed sequentially for the wholesome unraveling of self.

Keep this book handy to remind you at any time, should you forget, or need support to open up your bigger picture to resolve any situation, as we step through the nine portals of Remembering!

1. **Remembering – The Truth of Human Beings.**
    Reconnect with the innate intelligence and
    wholeness we were born with and recollect the
    soul's original blueprint.

2. **Driver's Seat – Realizing We Have Been Victims to
    Life.** Wake up from passive living and reclaim our
    power by releasing unconscious programming and
    switching from reaction to response.

3. **Natural Connection – Symbiosis of All Living
    Things.** Explore the sacred interconnectedness
    between all beings and our place within nature and
    the cosmic web of life.

4. **Untrue Belief Systems – Releasing Hidden
    Restrictions.**Bring unconscious beliefs and
    generational trauma into the light where healing
    begins through awareness, acceptance, and the
    courage to let go.

5. **Internal Senses – Listening to the Body's Wisdom.**
    Deepen into the language of the body by feeling,
    giving, receiving, and realigning through our inner
    sensory system of harmony.

6. **Communication – Effective Communication
    Changes Everything.** Learn the language of real
    communication and the power it holds to improve
    our lives.

7. **Challenges – Pathways Through Barriers.**
    Challenges as initiations to greater wisdom where
    a new version of self is available, as break*downs*
    become break*throughs*, and old patterns can be
    changed.

8. **Creativity – The Flow of Conscious Expression.**
   Where creativity exists and how to access
   inspiration, intuition, and flow as a way of life.

9. **Restoration Of Original Love – Connecting Our
   Spiritual Network.** Finding (and living) the truth of
   our unconditional love source.

When we choose to live life from the inside out, extraordinary benefits are available.

You will find that:

* Old negative mental patterns loosen their grip and their repetitive behaviors dissolve, as fresh, insightful knowingness starts to guide us forward.

* Our perspective widens and understanding of others increases. Guidance begins to arise not from fear-based thinking, but from gut instincts, intuition, and heart resonance.

* Life shifts from feeling flat and constrained to rich, dimensional, and alive.

* We move from separation and feeling isolated toward connection with all living things.

* We switch from feeling forced, to being in flow, off autopilot, to living in present time where energy is freely exchanged, not blocked and defended.

* We start to remember something essential about who we really are; that our true nature can't be confined. It has always been, and will always be rooted in the energy of freedom, truth and love.

If something in these pages resonates with you, it may be your own quiet tap on the shoulder, asking you the question, "Are you willing to let go...?"

Energy Matters!

Sometimes life doesn't unfold the way we imagined. In truth, it almost never does!

From an early age, we begin weaving dreams and visions shaped by what we see around us. We look outward, measuring the world, noticing what others have, their relationships, children, wealth, success, fame, and without realizing, we begin to reach for the same things, believing they will make us whole.

We chase images, roles, and ideals, hoping they'll fill the void within, but what if that space was never meant to be filled from the outside?

In a culture conditioned to go after what we want, we've lost touch with our deeper integrity. We've been led to believe that power comes from control; by forcing outcomes and accumulation, whether it is possessions, status, or visibility, without stopping and asking, "Is this right path for me?"

If we did, we would be tuning into our energy, intuition, and gut instincts and truly listening. This would remind us, *we are energy before we are matter*, and when this is remembered, our reality begins to shift.

The heart is our deepest energetic gateway and when it is freely open, this vibration carries a harmonic rhythm with life itself. We move out of the mind's duality of having or not having, into the unity of oneness, and being in tune. In other words, out of control and into flow, from survival to creation, and into alignment with the soul where our potential truly lies.

This book is not a physical map of 'How To'; rather, it's a guide to activate your internal compass, to play your authentic note in tune with the universal orchestra. It is the silent unknown between the words, where we start to pick up our tune, our mind releases its discord and our note becomes pure.

Here is a story to remind you...

Beyond the Illusion Story
- The Sound Of Home

The queues stretched endlessly, flickering with light. Souls gathered in silence, drawn to a call older than time itself – the whisper from Earth pulling them to return.

Lily turned to Gabe, her eternal companion across lifetimes, and her voice trembled with anticipation. "Do you feel it? Earth is calling us back. This is our chance, to complete what we started."

Gabe smiled faintly, though his gaze held the weight of countless returns. "I feel it, Lily. It's amazing to step into the density of a body again, to taste joy and heartbreak as if they were real, to forget, and then to remember once more."

He paused, his voice lowering to almost the rhythm of a prayer. "Last time, we got lost. We mistook survival for purpose, comfort for freedom, love for possession and we lost ourselves!"

Lily reached for his hand, feeling the stirring of anticipation vibrating all around them, thousands of souls readying themselves for their leap of faith. All prepared to answer Earth's calling as her deep frequency reverberated through the unseen layers of the universe, like the distant song of a whale calling its pod home.

Gabe tilted his head, listening. "She's letting go," he said softly. "And she's asking us to do the same. This time, Lily... we'll remember."

Lily felt her heart expand with a quiet knowing. "She's calling us into alignment," she murmured. "Back to the oneness we've always been."

Gabe turned to her, his voice steady and certain. "We understand more now. We know the game. We know how the collective mind traps us with survival, security, money, relationships, always triggering us into fear, making us collapse into stories that were never ours."

Lily smiled, though her eyes softened with memory. "I know. Last time, I thought I had it all. Fame, fortune, approval. I believed I was powerful because everyone told me I was. And then my body failed me. No amount of control could bring it back. It broke me... but maybe it woke me, too."

Gabe brushed his fingers across hers gently, his smile warm and timeless. "Sometimes it takes *breaking* to finally remember who we are."

All around them, the queues moved forward, souls stepping toward their chosen portals. The Earth Check-in Point shimmered ahead.

The Leap

Lily entered the Crosscheck Chamber, light cascading across her as she faced her 'take-off' questions. She tingled as she felt a galactic nod of approval for her courage and the timing of her mission.

"Have you chosen your mother? Your father? Your country? Do you agree to have your memory shut down on entry? " questioned the attendant.

"Yes," she replied, her voice steady. "I've made contact with both... and my landing point is Melbourne, Australia, and yes, I agree to have my memory shut down on entry and only to be reopened by my own remembering while on Planet Earth."

Her heart skipped as she spoke, knowing why she had made these choices.

Last time she had clung too tightly to her family story. She had loved, but her love became conditional, not inclusive, and bound by duty, instead of flowing with her inner truth. This time, she was choosing freedom and authenticity, no matter what others did.

Turning to Gabe, she placed her hand gently against his chest. "Goodbye, my precious one. We'll find each other, and this time, we'll remember."

He held her gaze, infinite and unwavering. "You will find me, Lily, and I will find you. We are never separate."

And then — **whoosh** — she was gone!

New Beginnings

Lily opened her newborn eyes to soft breath and the warmth of skin. Her mother cradled her against her bare chest, tears in her eyes as she whispered gently:

"Welcome, my beautiful girl.
Thank you for choosing me."

Lily's tiny heart swelled as she thought; "This time is different, my mother is awake and my father is, too! I can feel love present from the very beginning!"

Across Australia in the city of Perth, Gabe's entry was harder.

His mother's body trembled with fear, her breath shallow, her mind spiraling. Gabe tried to soothe her with his love frequency, but moments later, bright lights engulfed him. Cold air, hard surfaces, strange hands moving him with rough urgency, where was he?

"This isn't what I expected!" Panic was rising as he reminded himself, "Stay awake, don't forget, don't forget her!"

He was placed in a humidicrib, separated from his mother, feeling her grief ripple through the sterile walls that contained his tiny body he vowed to give his love to her as part of his mission! "What was the other part of my mission?" he frantically asked himself.

Two souls, two different beginnings, two stories unfolding into vastly different experiences...

One purpose transcending time and space, to remember who we truly are, is the mission possible?

Beyond the Illusion

What if this isn't just Lily and Gabe's story?

What if it's your story? Everyone's story?

What if, lifetime after lifetime, we've been caught in a grand illusion, believing we are separate from each other, from love, from life, from ourselves?

Somewhere along the way, we started to believe our power comes from having, accumulating, achieving, and controlling, however, that belief is the illusion itself.

Real power comes from remembering who we are, beyond the perceived storyline we are taught!

First Remembering Opens!

The power of unconditional love grants sovereignty and exists in all of us. It relates to holding the expansive conscious reality, whilst enjoying being part of it through our life story. It's the non-attachment to anything, yet the enjoyment of everything! It's about freedom to exist outside the mind's restriction!

We are here within a physical body to have real earthly experiences, whatever that means to each and every one of us. Some may choose to explore human being potential by discovering hidden upsets buried deep within that have inhibited self-realization, or others may choose a different course.

I've chosen to explore and it has taken me many years to unwind and get a sense of my way home! I'm still following this infinite inner guidance, however I'm now coming from a completely different place than I was years ago. Somehow I seem to be ahead of my physical self and willing to keep moving forwards into the unknown, towards a familiar energy patiently waiting to be remembered!

I share with you my raw personal stories from where I was in earlier times, living without the awareness I now have. It's to demonstrate the ability we all have to move ourselves through any challenge to a greater, more expansive truth.

Many of us have forgotten we are more than a physical body. We are also unseen energy that powers and supports our 'solid' physical state.

The more we are aware of this, the greater our capacity to manifest a joyful and authentic life.

This book supports remembering and further opening our soul, spirit, higher self, or heart-centered intelligence energy for you to find your original note. By traveling through nine transformative gateways, each one expands awareness as we let go and open to increased understanding of our true self.

With these realizations, we start to 'join the dots' which stabilizes this greater field and allows our natural consciousness to flow, bringing lighter, brighter richness and meaning to life even while navigating challenges.

You will be surprised, confronted, and delighted as you move through these gateways to acknowledge the bigger picture of our human being-ness and what it means to be part of humanity at this time.

What have I learned?

Love is not something we are meant to go looking for externally. It's found within!

We live in a crazy world where as children, few of us are taught the basic fundamental premise that *we are love.* We are energetic beings within a physical body. Therefore our natural source currency to be exchanged is love.

Alternatively, we are conditioned to think that we need to earn love in order to be valued. *Do you know, the hardest thing in the world to do, is to unconditionally love yourself?* When we have learned that, we expand that love to all.

If we carried the truth of our original energy we would not be separate from anything, and we'd understand how life intuitively flows for all sentient beings.

Nature teaches us about energetic resonance, a tree is a tree for example, and doesn't try and be anything else; no matter the weather, circumstances or human acknowledgment, it constantly remains true to itself. The same can be said for a bee, a cow, or a flower. All are in synchronicity with their internal and external realities.

As conscious human beings we have separated from our natural ability to *be* and have sought the answers with our minds' intellect without really knowing that we are caught in a physical, linear game. The only way for us to come out, is to go in, and find the truth for ourselves, not via the intellect, but rather, through *feeling* and opening our heart resonance to remember.

So how do we do this?

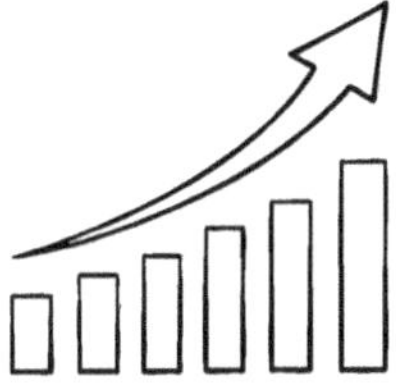

Where Did It All Start?

Before we dive into the enriching process of unraveling our personal untruths and reclaiming deeper ones, it's worth taking a moment to reflect on the tools and pathways that have guided us toward greater consciousness over the modern decades.

This isn't just nostalgia, it's a way of honoring our collective evolution and seeing how, as our awareness grows, so too does our relationship with all life. Everything is shifting, always and we're beginning to feel that, not just intellectually, but experiencing this as global change.

There was a time not so long ago when inner work felt like trudging through wet cement. Uncovering old blocks, healing patterns and shifting negative mindsets took years. It was heavy, slow, and often lonely work. However now, we're standing on the edge of a different energetic field entirely. The influx of light from solar flares, mass coronal ejections, the Earth's passage through the photon belt, and the intricate dance of planetary alignments are all contributing to support a massive shift.

This isn't just 'woo woo', this is truth, felt in the bodies and hearts of many people, as well as scientifically proven by the academic world: Dr. David Clements (Physicist, Oxford and Cambridge Universities), Nassim Haramein (Physicist), Greg Bradden (Geologist/Scientist) and many more.

We are living in a convergence of time, energy, resonance and cosmic orchestration, which is helping us crack open outdated hierarchies and false systems. What once held power over us, and kept us believing we couldn't make a difference, is now being exposed and dismantled as we rise into the truth of who we are as human beings.

Something entirely new is asking to be born and we're not just witnessing it, we're orchestrating it!

Self-Help Through the Decades

My fascination with the esoteric and spiritual began as a teenager.

My mum and I would often go to clairvoyants, psychics, tarot readers, and astrologers to find out what might be in the cards for us.

I remember a number of them said I was going to meet a sailor named 'Terry' who was sailing around the world. Every time I'd meet someone, I'd ask if their name was Terry. Sadly it wasn't, and I'm still yet to meet him!

This was the '80s, when personal development was opening up and beginning to be commercialized by a plethora of knowledgeable and connected souls.

Humanity, long looking for answers could suddenly access limitless information from these sages and insightful human beings.

There are simply too many wonderful ones to list, however these books in particular have supported me through different times in my life:

* *You Can Heal Your Life* – Louise Hay

* *Your Erroneous Zones* – Wayne Dyer

* *The Power of Now* – Eckhart Tolle

* *The Prophet* – Kahlil Gibran

* *Nature, Man and Woman* – Alan Watts

* *The Way of the Peaceful Warrior* – Dan Millman

* *The Alchemist* – Paulo Coelho

* *The Four Agreements* – Don Miguel Ruiz

* *The Celestine Prophecy* – James Redfield

* *Astrology For The Soul* – Jan Spiller

* *The Astrology Of Fate* – Liz Greene

* *The Field* – Lyn McTaggart

* *Don't Sweat The Small Stuff* – Richard Carlson

* *The Seat Of The Soul* – Gary Zukav

* *The Turning Point* – Gregg Braden

* *The Untethered Soul* – Michael Singer

* *Conversations With God* – Neale Donald Walsch

* *The Road Less Travelled* – M. Scott Peck

* *Dying To Be Me* – Anita Moorjani

* *The Creative Act* – Rick Rubin

* *The Tibetan Book Of Living & Dying* – Sogyal Rinpoche

There are so many influential writers who shared ground-breaking information, too many to mention, however all are acknowledged for every genuine word written and their contribution to expanding the field of human consciousness.

A Snapshot of Self-Help/Spiritual Evolution

* **Humanistic Psychology (1960-1970)** – Focused on personal growth, self-actualization, and the power of positive thinking.

* **New Age Spirituality (1970-1980)** – Explored spirituality beyond traditional religious boundaries, incorporating meditation, energy healing, channeling and tools such as runes, oracle and affirmation card decks.

* **Mindfulness and Presence (1990-2000s)** – Emphasized living in the present moment, reducing stress, and discovering inner peace through the clearing of negativity.

* **Integration of Neuroscience & Emotional Intelligence (2000-2010)** – Brought scientific understanding to self-help. Taught us that we can re-wire our brains through neuroplasticity.

* **Digital Age and Online Communities (2010-2020)** – Law of Attraction popularized. Sharing became communal as well as global.

* **Emotional and Mental Healing/Counselling/AI (2020)** – Increasing consciousness of our universal connection.

Body and Healing

The 1980s and 1990s marked a quiet revolution in the way we approached health – not just as physical fitness, but as a full-body return to wholeness. It was about the mind and spirit, as well as the body.

From Iyengar's disciplined alignment to Kundalini's awakening flows, yoga was no longer just stretching, it became an inward portal for healing.

People started to wonder if healing wasn't merely physical. This sparked a wave of interest in energetic and vibrational therapies. Reiki and Pranic healing emerged as gentle, hands-on (or hands-above) modalities that worked with the body's energy field to shift blockages and restore flow. Color therapy, chakra balancing, and theta healing followed, offering new ways to understand how emotions, memories, and even thought patterns could affect health and consciousness.

Underpinning the New Age were practices like Transcendental Meditation, mindfulness and guided visualization which offered stillness and connection in a fast-paced world.

Breathwork also bridged the gap between body and soul. Modalities like Rebirthing and Transformational Breathwork showed that the breath could access what words could not.

A wide field of complementary tools emerged. Sound healing with crystal bowls, gongs and mantras brought vibrational shifts through resonance. We began to pay attention to the significance of frequency. It was also the time we realized the importance of our inner-child and stopped the reliance on living in our minds.

Part of our awakening brought a deeper attunement to the way we nourished our bodies. We began to question not just what we ate, but the energy, quality, and intention behind our food and drink whilst developing a stronger symbiosis with all of life.

Plant-based living emerged not as a trend, but as a conscious, harmonious choice, aligned with compassion and vitality. Alongside this, came a profound awareness of the importance of purified water, and its sacred role in cleansing, energizing, and sustaining vitality.

These approaches combined to form a powerful, intuitive language of transformation.

As we moved through the 2000s to the present day, it's been a time when healing became deeply personal, spiritual, and embodied. We stopped looking 'out there' and began listening 'in here'. The body became a messenger, the nervous system, a communicator, and the distinction between our external and internal worlds softened.

People didn't just want to feel better – they sought to awaken, to remember who they truly are, and to live consciously in symbiosis with life.

I have read many self-help books and dabbled in most of the healing modalities over the years. I operated like a giant sponge, totally engaged with the 'energetics', rather than the 'matter' of life. I'd always be looking for cause, not just accepting symptoms, so everything went through a filter whereby I'd absorb what resonated with me at the time, and discard the rest.

I was obsessed with disciplines like Reiki, Pranic Healing and Astrology. The former really helped my family many years ago when my mum was dying. We knew a Grand Reiki Master and she came to our family home and taught my dad, sister, and two brothers about Reiki to help ease her loss and pain and support our family connection. It was an amazingly beautiful experience for us all.

It was an energetic way we could offer support as we had no physical control over what was happening and all felt hopeless around that. Our love really comforted Mum, as we were all totally invested in her care.

I remember often lying on her bed and spooning into her back. I'd place my hands wherever they needed to go as I was guided by something much greater, which seemed to be from 'out of this world', I guess it also came from within as ONE LOVE came together for her, me and the entire family.

It certainly feels like this isn't our first time here and perhaps we arrive each lifetime carrying threads from the past, unfinished moments, emotional imprints, and lessons still waiting to be understood. These lineages aren't here to weight us down, they are 'sounds of guidance' to wake us up.

Imagine the soul as a radiant, original design, pure, whole, and complete. However, as we move through life after life, it's like making photocopies of that original. Each copy fades just a little, until eventually we forget what we once knew. We lose connection to that deeper part of ourselves and begin to live only on the surface by prioritizing thinking, doing, achieving and controlling.

That forgetting pulls us into a slower, heavier way of living. We can feel it as the body tightens, the mind becomes contrary and spins us into confusion. We then need to rely on structure, certainty, and stories to stabilize us and to solely believe in the proven, seen, tangible world.

However, in this world, there is always something missing. We continue to carry a quiet moral compass of knowing, albeit subtle. Even when life looks 'good', there is a strange emptiness and perhaps a quiet inner voice whispering, "I know there's more than this!"

Thank goodness for that whisper as it helps us remember there is more to life than chasing relationships, status, wealth, or recognition as they are all external ways of filling up. The satisfaction they bring is always temporary! So how do we fill ourselves up from the inside?

It's like running a race we invented, scattering dozens of invisible flags across the sand and declaring; "Only when I collect all these flags will I be enough!" So we place our value on outside accomplishment, rather than the understanding that we are already good enough!

Our inner voice is louder now as it reminds us we are not just physical bodies, we are energetic beings living in a connected, unified field, and everything that we do creates a ripple effect. This isn't just a spiritual ideology; many learned physicists are now proving the quantum field of this frequency is undeniable.

> *"Nassim posits that the universe is fundamentally comprised of consciousness and that all matter, energy, and information are entangled within a quantum field. From this perspective, an individual's emotional states, particularly those associated with love, can be seen as frequencies that influence their personal 'antenna' (the heart/brain system) and their interaction with this universal field."*– Nassim Haramein – Renowned Theoretical Physicist

I met Nassim some years ago in Byron Bay at a friend's house for a small gathering. While seated together I casually asked him, "What do you think about the energy of love?" His answer was similar to what I've already shared, however, I sense that in the ensuing years, he'd have discovered far more evidence to support his theory.

We are not talking about love as emotion, but love as a state of coherence, a felt alignment between who we truly are and how we show up in the world. When we drop out of the mind's state of overthinking and into the clarity of heart resonance, something shifts. We stop resisting and start flowing with natural symbiosis.

This makes it easier for us to let go of control and those old uncomfortable patterns that regularly arise and keep us stuck. All that is happening is we are releasing the discomfort of the tension between who we've been, and who we're becoming.

Meeting these old patterns with curiosity instead of judgment helps to easily untangle them as many of these threads may have been knotted for lifetimes. As we loosen the knots through awareness, the tension releases and the bond frees itself.

This unraveling opens the flow for everything to change; our body relaxes, our mind clears and our heart resonance opens to align with our true nature.

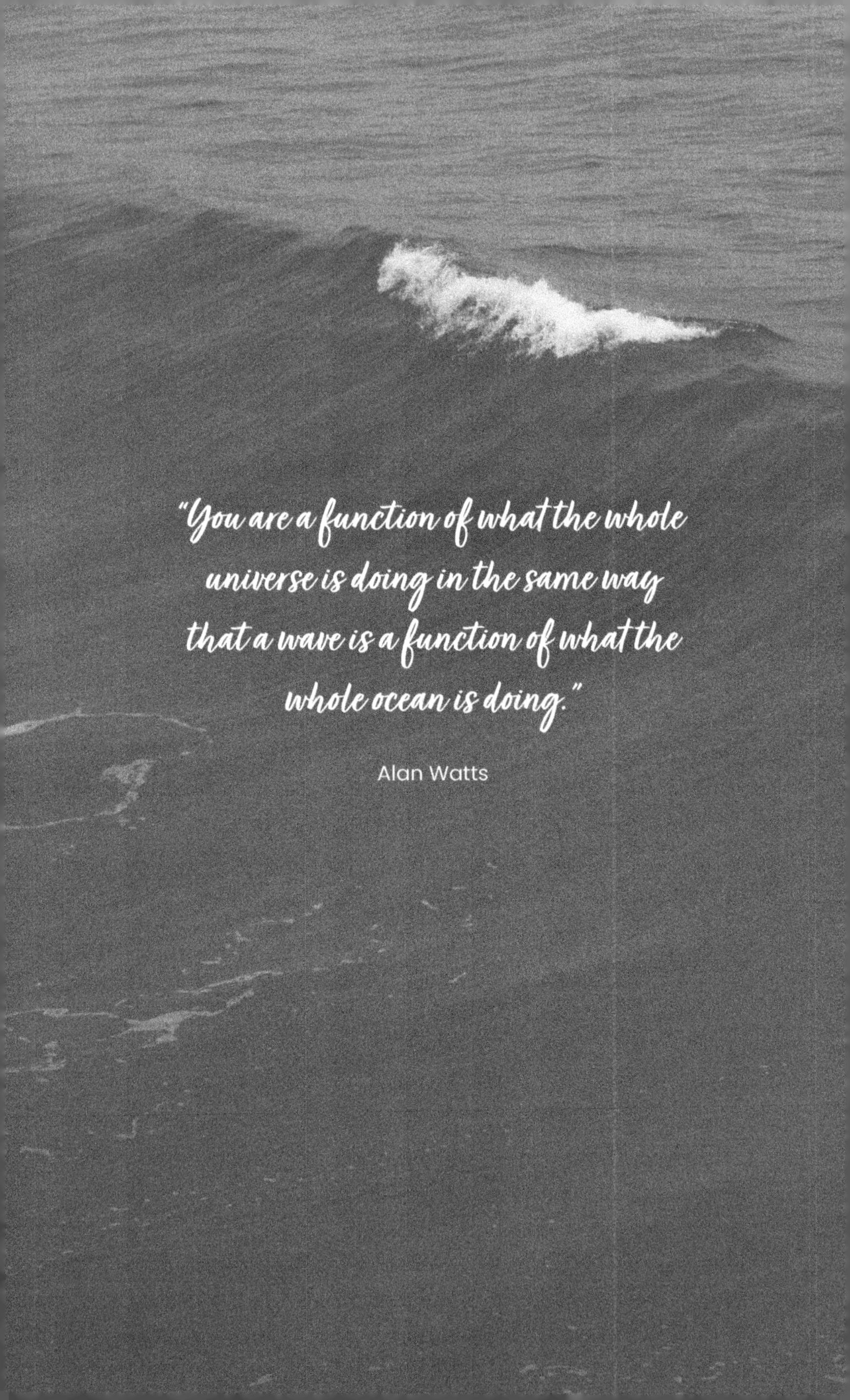

"You are a function of what the whole universe is doing in the same way that a wave is a function of what the whole ocean is doing."

Alan Watts

Remembering

The Truth of Human Beings

Big Picture

From the moment we are born, we are taught to seek ourselves in the mirror of others.

We quickly learn that if our mum smiles, we must be good, and if our dad withdraws, we've done something wrong. Praise becomes proof of worth, and this mindset makes us desperately seek approval as a way of validating our existence. By constantly looking outwards for our value we quickly become conditioned to operating in the mind's duality of good vs bad and right vs wrong, where our performance becomes a measure of feeling loved or feeling worthless.

Our parents were not told and nor did they tell us that simply 'being' our natural self is enough. It is the beginning point of life. The power of being present with our internal world, by default, creates our external one. Feelings are our Geiger counter, and whether good or bad, we need to feel and release them, so they are not pushed down and stored in the mind and body.

Our parents didn't tell us, because it was never said to them, "You are here because you chose to be here. We are so happy you chose us and we will help you to remember, to heal, to feel your way through your experiences so you can have your own adventures while walking through the illusion and finding your way home."

Instead, we teach our children to look outside themselves and to learn to be reactive to life. To protect through forming barriers, to chase meaning through action, productivity, perfection and to barricade themselves in, often to become someone they are not.

When we experience negative actions against us, we get hurt, feel uncomfortable and can become resentful, thinking there is something wrong with us. To feel okay again, we push the feeling down which creates a little knot inside and we continue to do this every time we feel emotionally uncomfortable. The first step is for us to undo the knots so we can start to feel comfortable with being ourselves again.

 *Personal Experience*

The Lost Compass

If someone had told me in my younger years when I was full of dreams, ambitions and a strong desire to 'make it' in life, that the greatest adventure would not be outward, but inward, I would have laughed in disbelief.

Back then success meant being seen, shining brightly, and being loved for how well I could perform the role that was expected of me. I wore my shiny skills on the outside hoping they would be enough to earn connection and approval, never realizing the quiet emptiness I carried underneath. The more applause I received, the further away I travelled from my inner truth.

I gravitated to work environments that rewarded those skills that reinforced the belief I needed to be what others wanted me to be, in order to be accepted. My emotions and real feelings were pushed down so far I convinced myself they didn't exist.

From the outside I looked highly successful, but on the inside I was lost. I became a woman living in two worlds, the outside one polished and validated by money, achievement and things that looked good, the other, longing for truth, integrity and love. I told myself it was okay as it looked as though everyone was doing the same thing.

There were times I tried to escape by numbing out and drinking too much, pretending that it meant freedom and that fun would fill me up, however it did the opposite, it made me feel hollow inside and magnified the ache.

Life has a way of stripping back the layers and through heartbreak, loneliness and fear I was finally cracked open and realized I was ready to let those cracks shine light into my darkness and direct me to where I needed to heal.

For years I believed I was building a happy and successful life and to an extent I was, however, those cracks illuminated a messy, raw, and real inner world. Beneath achievement and approval seeking, I found my fearful little girl, longing to be loved, not for her performance, but simply for who she was.

The truth uncovered was both painful and liberating and lead me to wanting to discover more. To acknowledge my little girl and integrate her into my heart as the oneness we had always been.

Eventually I learned what I wish someone had told me a long time ago.

Love is not earned, it's not won, it doesn't live in performance, it lies within, quietly waiting to be remembered.

As I wrote about these early years I became more aware that we all carry misunderstood stories. Some of us keep them forever buried while others reach a point where we begin to wake up and are ready to be honest with ourselves, possibly for the first time.

As you read these pages I invite you to reflect on where you are in your own story. Are you still carrying your misunderstood self quietly within? Or are you ready to look inward, even if it's a little messy, to discover what's on the other side and the freedom the truth holds for you?

I share with you the raw patterns and effects of my behaviors for further insight.

 *Patterns*

* Not good enough/no belief in self

* Value money over wholesome love

* Constantly comparing personal lack against others' wealth (scarcity thinking)

* Jealousy and competitiveness

* Buried emotions and suppressed intuition

 *Effects*

* Constant loop of 'Trying to be the best – failing – not good enough – trying harder- failing again'

* The need for control developed a 'harsh inner critic' who showed no love towards self, only harshness for failure

* Separation between self and others, by being controlled by the mind

* Living superficial life created superficial relationships resulting in inner loneliness

World of Duality

As children, we begin life bright and open, feeling everything. Over time, without even realizing it, we start collecting the thoughts and energies of others. Unspoken doubts, quiet criticisms, and disappointments that weren't ours, somehow become part of our story.

Then something happens, an experience that hurts, confuses, or frightens us and in that moment, a belief is formed. *"I'm not good enough." "I'm not safe." "Something's wrong with me."* These beliefs take root because something real occurred in the physical world and we believe the feeling must be true as the pain supports this perception.

Often, these are the moments when we felt vulnerable, confused, or unseen. We didn't know how to process what was happening and we wanted to feel better so we pushed down the discomfort, hid the pain and told ourselves we're okay, when we were not.

As mentioned before, most of us were not taught what to *do* with uncomfortable emotions. No one told us it was okay to feel them, let alone that emotions were meant to move, not stay stuck. When we allow ourselves to feel with awareness, not judgment, emotion becomes **energy in motion (e-motion)** and will naturally shift and heal.

Instead, we learn to chase the feel-good chemicals and become addicted to joy, success, and certainty. This causes an inner division between 'good feelings' and 'bad feelings'. One we chase, the other, we avoid!

This duality becomes the lens through which we engage with the world.

From there, we build personal bubbles around us to hide our feelings. These invisible bubbles are made of protection, preference, and performance. We speak to others from our 'good experience bubble', saying whatever will make us be liked, seen, or approved of, so we can control others' perceptions of us, rather than act with transparent authenticity.

We end up with people talking *at* each other, not *with* each other. Everyone carefully protecting their inner world, trying to control how they feel, seeking good feelings and avoiding discomfort and the result is a world full of people craving connection, yet causing separation.

The only way to liberate ourselves is to burst our bubble! To truly free ourselves from these protective patterns is to come back to our heart, not through analysis or intellect, but through feeling.

For instance, intellectually saying, *"I know I shut down when I'm upset,"* might offer insight, however without emotional release the energy doesn't change, and the same pattern will keep repeating.

When we meet these hidden emotional layers with presence and compassion and allow the discomfort to be felt, rather than fixed, we pop the bubble and a shift occurs where people feel our authenticity where words and energy match.

Over time, when emotions are unfelt and unacknowledged, they build up, layer upon layer, until we become numb to our feelings and the feelings of others. Numbness isn't a flaw, its protection, however, when we stay numb, we live entirely in the mind.

We cling to logic and endeavor to control outcomes. We believe the physical world is all there is, measurable, linear, and safe.

In that world view, there's no room for magic. No space for curiosity, and our heart intelligence, the very center of our human experience, remains silent and unheard.

This isn't how we're meant to live. We are not here to only stay safe and secure, we are here to experience, explore, learn and grow, to find out what we don't know, not what we do!

 *Client Story*

This is my recollection of what happened recently in one of my personal face-to-face one hour sessions which the client has approved to be shared here.

I counseled a teenage boy who was devastated that his mother had not picked him up spiritually as a child, when he believed he had picked her up all his life.

He shared how he had always known what was happening but recognized he had to do it in her 'conditional, physical' way to get her love. If he rocked the boat with different opinions she would take it personally and become the victim to his words.

He didn't want to hurt her or get into trouble, so he stopped expecting to be understood and knew it was his job to understand her.

Having been divorced for many years, his mother had found a new man that her son didn't get along with. He thought his mum was totally losing herself in the relationship and felt abandoned and unloved by her as a consequence.

He believed with this new relationship that his mother had broken their agreement of always being together and connected.

This had raised deep resentment, and he shared what he claimed he had done for her in the past, and now she was making crazy decisions, and becoming more controlling!

I worked with him around his belief systems and zeroed in on one that had become a core value he was holding on to. It was, **"If I let go of her, she'll change and I'll lose her!"**

I started digging into this belief by asking, "What would be the possible outcome of any situation with you holding that belief?" He replied, **"If I let go of her, she'll change and I'll lose her!"** *This young man is very aware and his immediate realization surprised me!*

"OMG!" he said. "My mum thinks the same thing I do; we're mirroring each other...she believes **'If I let go of him, he'll change and I'll lose him!'"**

"I had no idea I was doing this to her! I'm not trusting her to find her own way, to make her own decisions, to be her own person...ultimately to be free, not controlled or attached to anyone, just free to be and the truth remains... in the freedom of our mother/son connection!"

I'm finding with many of my current sessions there is heaviness, along with controlling energy, particularly around relationships, finances and health, which is taking people to the point of hopelessness.

It is important for us to stay very present, not to go into overthinking or old ways of problem solving, as it locks in repetitive patterns that no longer work. The following exercises offer support to change these patterns and to help you start to remember.

Exercises

How do I gain the most from completing each gateway exercise?

* It is recommended you find a notebook or journal to write your thoughts and awarenesses as you adventure through these transformative gateways, as reflection will be helpful on completion of the book.

* Keep it by your bedside and jot down intuitive notes when you feel inspired to do so. Often early in the morning is a great time as the mind is passive and feelings are easier to access.

* Give yourself time to do the exercises, ideally 15-30 mins to tune in to your inner senses and write from the unknown, rather than the known.

* Don't do the exercises when you feel moody, distracted or out of sorts, unless you are willing to change how you want to feel. The best results will happen when your intention is open to the process of change.

* The space required is quiet, where you can tune in to your breath, let go of whatever you have been doing and with curiosity, start reading the exercise through once. Then go to the first point and complete each step with your head and heart open to all possibilities.

* If you feel drawn to do any gateway or exercise out of sequence this is great, as you are intuitively feeling where you need to go first to unwind. Also, if you find any exercise too tedious, just let it go and come back to it when you feel ready.

✳ The best way to work through the pages is to keep flowing, rather than getting stuck on any particular gateway. You can always revisit after you have completed the book with greater understanding.

 *Gateway One*

Remembering Exercises

Tuning in to Early Behavioral Patterns

1. Conscious Choice Check-In

Purpose: *Shift stuck patterns through small, empowered choices.*

✳ Sit quietly with pen and paper, take a few grounding breaths.

✳ Reflect on where you feel stuck, frustrated, or powerless, e.g. *"I'm always trying to please people."*

✳ Ask yourself; *"Where am I waiting for someone else to change their behavior so I don't have to please them all the time?"* e.g. *"I'm always looking for my partner to acknowledge me and he/she doesn't!"*

✳ Describe the situation honestly and how it affects you? e.g. *"I need validation from them as I don't believe or trust myself."*

✳ Gently explore; *"What conscious choices can I make to improve my life?"* e.g. *"I could stop seeking their approval as that restricts me and my approval of me."*

✳ List a few small, empowering actions available to you now, e.g. *"I could trust myself more and listen without feeling I have to always agree. If they have negative feedback, I should be open and curious rather than defensive. It is just their opinion."* Circle the actions you feel ready to commit to this week.

* Know that these small awarenesses and aligned actions begin to shift energy and bring us out of our automatic reactive responses, into more aligned new ones.

2. My Old Agreement

Purpose: *Release outdated beliefs and create new supportive ones.*

* Breathe deeply and settle into a reflective state.

* Tune into a belief or pattern you may have, e.g. *"I don't like being vulnerable."*

* Ask yourself, *"When did I first take this on, and what circumstance made me do that?"* e.g. mother's anger, father's absence.

* Write down the original inner agreement, e.g. *"Not safe to be vulnerable!"*

* Acknowledge how it once served or protected you, e.g. *"It hurts less if I avoid my feelings!"*

* Ask yourself; *"Is this still true for who I am now?"* e.g. *"No, I want to feel my emotion, be real and more wholesome, be myself, warts and all!"*

* Write a new inner agreement that supports your growth e.g. *"When I feel vulnerable I let myself feel uncomfortable and breathe before responding, as I keep feeling my way through the emotion!"*

   ENERGY MATTERS!

* Sit with the shift — feel the freedom of your awareness.

3. The Mirror Moment

Purpose: *Use triggers as a mirror for self-awareness and growth.*

* Think of someone who triggers you emotionally.

* Note what exactly bothers you about their behavior, e.g. *"They are always critical of me."*

* Ask yourself; *"What is this showing me about myself?"* e.g. *"Am I critical of others?"*

* Consider whether it reflects something unacknowledged within you, e.g. *"I am judgmental of others."*

* Write honestly about the insight or lesson e.g. *"If I'm judgmental of others are they going to be judgmental of me, and what can I do to listen without judgment?"*

* Ask yourself; *"What shift can I make within me?"* e.g. *"Rather than judging the negative, I could listen objectively with curiosity."*

* Note one new way to respond next time it arises and what that would look like e.g. *"Need to have an intention to stay present and ask open questions for clarification so that we can come together and not be separate."*

* Give heartfelt thanks to the vision of you in the mirror for helping you to grow.

4. Releasing Through Awareness

Purpose: *Own your part, let go and find your power.*

* Focus on a situation where you feel disempowered –
  e.g. *"I feel my boss never listens to me!"*

* Describe the experience and how it impacts you, e.g.
  *"Before I meet him I already have an expectation that he
  won't be listening to anything I have to say."*

* Make a decision — this marks a turning point – e.g.
  Change needs to happen from me.

* Now ask; *"What part of this is mine to own?"* e.g. *"I have
  a negative expectation on him that he doesn't value me,
  that's why he doesn't listen!"*

* Write your part without blame, thoughts, reactions,
  boundaries – e.g. *"It is my lack of value of myself and
  judging him on what I think, not knowing what he really
  thinks."*

* Acknowledge what's yours and let the rest go, e.g.
  *"The whole thing is my creation to let go of and start a
  fresh relationship, based on my value and willingness to
  connect freely beyond anyone's judgments."*

* Finish with: *"My awareness expands by taking
  responsibility for the part I played in creating this
  situation."*

* Sit with the energy of expansion and freedom and
  in this 'new' awareness you will instinctively know
  your next steps. Write them down.

5. Reclaiming My Power

Purpose: *Uncovering the truth of you.*

* Sit quietly with your eyes closed and take a few deep, calming breaths.

* Sense where in your life you've been letting outside forces or old fears direct your choices.

* Gently name what you've been handing your power over to, whether it's a person, belief, emotion, or story e.g. *"My mum, my dad, my first teacher, my boyfriend, my boss, etc."*

* Imagine lovingly gathering your negative energy back from each of these people. *"I need to let go of my judgments of my mum's behavior as she was upset, in her own bubble and totally unaware!"*

* Feel yourself standing in the center of your own being-ness, calm, steady, and awake. Ask yourself: *"What truth do I now choose to live by?"* e.g. *"Around my mum/boss/teacher?"* and write it down.

Write in your journal how you feel after doing your 'Gateway One – Remembering' exercises as it gives a sense of where you are now, and what can change in the next moment.

"I am not what happened to me.
I am what I choose to become."

Carl Jung

GATEWAY TWO

The Driver's Seat

*Realizing We Have Been
Passengers In Life*

 ***Big Picture***

We grow up learning to behave a certain way and are rewarded for it. If we follow the 'right' path, as set out by others, we'll be accepted and without realizing it, we give our power away to external forces. We become conditioned to believe life is something that happens to us, rather than something we create!

Let's look in the rear vision mirror of our life and see when we've been riding along as passengers and blamed the driver for where we ended up!

One of the biggest reasons so many of us feel off track, stuck, frustrated, or powerless, is because we've been conditioned to look outside ourselves for both the cause of, and solutions to, our problems.

Unconsciously we start to become dependent on everything changing outside before we can feel okay. If someone hurts us, we shut off and blame them for the way we feel. Until *they* change, nothing can change.

By adulthood these beliefs run deep and blame is part of life. We blame the economy, partners, parents, bosses, even our children for not delivering what we want. It is much easier to blame than to take self-responsibility for the experiences we have created.

This is how we end up in the passenger seat of life. We hand control over to circumstances, routines, expectations, and other people's opinions. We react to what's happening around us instead of creating what we truly want. At times life can feel like a series of unpleasant detours we didn't choose, roads we didn't map and destinations that take us a long way from home.

On the surface this can appear perfectly normal as most of us are living this way. However many feel a relentless emptiness within that something is missing. Even if on the surface we are happy, we question; "Is that all there is?"

Transformation begins when we shift our focus from pointing outward to inward, and start owning, instead of blaming. This isn't about beating ourselves up! No, it's about recognizing we are responsible for our choices, beliefs, energy, and actions, which shape the life we are living.

With this awareness, we take back the wheel and drive in the direction that feels most authentic and real. However it's not always easy and means questioning long-held stories and beliefs we've created and inherited.

It means coming out of automatic pilot mode and being present with the negative thoughts that have affected self and others. We have unknowingly – or knowingly – hurt people, ourselves, and not taken responsibility for our actions.

If we want the negative energy to release, we need to be willing to feel, understand and care about what that hurt felt like for others, and ourselves, as a consequence of our thoughts and actions.

Some may think; *"Why should I do that? They hurt me first!"* However, it takes one person to open up the truer connection beyond mindset behaviors. As human beings we have all been trapped in the physical duality field of right and wrong which makes us judge others, rather than being curious to explore how we can harmonize our different viewpoints.

This raises our integrity and the only place we're truly in the driver's seat is with our heart resonance – that's our engine room! From this source we are able to see ourselves and others, beyond our everyday behavior, and realize that all human beings really want, is to connect, as that is our true nature.

Our lives have never been out of our hands, we just believed they were and the moment we truly understand and dispel this belief is the moment everything changes. As our inner world starts to align, our outer world begins to shift and ignites the process of dissolving old negative patterns to expose a clearer pathway forward.

We were never meant to be passengers; we were born to drive!

Outcome of Driving Experience: As a passenger we can always blame the driver for not ending up where we wanted to go. It is up to us to take the wheel of self-responsibility and head in the direction we feel to travel as the creator of our life experiences.

Head in the Sand

The moment I truly had to climb into the driver's seat of my life came with the ending of my 20-year marriage. Until then, I had been cocooned in a life of material comfort. We had built wealth, lived with ease, and for most of that adventure, I never had to worry about bills, finances, or the cost of anything. My husband handled all of that. We had a joint bank account, but I never laid eyes on it, nor did I ask to.

I remember the day he called me from a motor show. He said; "I want to buy a Maserati—what do you think?" Without hesitation, I replied; "John, if we can afford it, go for it, you deserve it!"

Looking back, that moment summed up so much. I had given away my power, trusting someone else to steer the vehicle of our shared life, without ever truly understanding where we were headed and with what.

When the financial tsunami hit after our separation, it didn't just sweep through his world, it crashed through mine as well! Suddenly, I found myself at 55, with very little money, no home, and no choice but to navigate a financial world I'd never taken the time to understand.

It would've been easy to blame him, to sink into resentment or regret. But in the quiet moments, I saw the truth... I hadn't stepped up. I had opted out of our financial reality. I held the belief that I didn't want to over-borrow money, however, he believed in leveraging debt. He was the CEO, smart and strategic, so I deferred to him.

The deeper truth was, I didn't trust myself, as I believed I had to understand finances in order to have a valid opinion.

This was my turning point.

Healthy relationships, especially those built on shared resources, need open, transparent conversations around money. Without that it's like driving blindfolded, eventually, you *will* crash.

I had to face the uncomfortable truth of my own avoidance. The denial, the fantasy that I could stay untouched by the consequences of choices I didn't make, but those I never really questioned.

Of course there was pain, but nevertheless, there was also liberation. I realized that true freedom came not from being taken care of, but from taking full responsibility, for my life, my choices, my healing. Slowly, I began to build a new relationship with money. One where I valued it, rather than feared or avoided it, I started to ask myself tough questions:

Do I really need this? Or am I trying to soothe something deeper inside me?

The road wasn't easy. But it was real. And that made all the difference.

I'm still creating my financial foundation, but I've never felt freer. My values have changed. They've realigned with my deeper nature, with integrity, simplicity and sovereignty. And while I may not yet have the material wealth I once did, what I do have is an inner richness that no amount of money could ever buy.

 *Patterns*

* Easy come, easy go attitude to money

* Gave freely and often, but struggled to receive

* Imbalance created a subtle control dynamic, where giving became a way to feel valued or safer

* Buried greater understanding of what money represented, which disconnected me from financial responsibility

Effects

* Unbalanced relationships where giving was expected and often taken for granted

* Lack of clear boundaries which made it difficult to establish mutual respect

* Others became reliant on me, which reinforced my supposed value

* Created surface-level connections, where genuine reciprocity was missing

* Approval-seeking became default behavior, which limited authenticity

Driven By Fear

Every time something goes wrong or we find ourselves in pain, disappointment, or conflict, we're standing at a choice point. Do we slip back into old patterns of blame, denial, frustration, self-criticism, or do we pause and ask ourselves a deeper question; *"What part did I play in this creation?"*

This question is asked of every client at some stage in their session as it relates to being able to take responsibility for creating our life and the degree that we can is commensurate to the degree change is possible. It's only our mind that believes this is not possible.

When we're willing to be vulnerable and communicate our feelings for the purpose of wanting to change our situation or find greater understanding, it releases 'stuck' emotional energy that has held us hostage. The moment we look inwards we expand our space, and gain clarity and understanding by releasing the blame we have held toward others, as well as ourselves.

When we fully immerse ourselves in the driver's seat, we begin to move beyond the old duality game of right and wrong, good and bad. We stop judging each experience and start being more curious to discover the truth, rather than being right. Life becomes less about control and perfection and, more about mindful experiences and being awake!

So how do we get out of the passenger seat? Let's say your relationship ends and you think; *"I'm never going to trust men again. I gave everything I had. I did everything right and it still wasn't enough!"* Yes, the physical pain is real, and when we allow ourselves to feel this in our body, without putting context or stories around the feeling, we have an access point for a deeper truth to emerge.

By asking the question; *"What part did I play in this creation?"* e.g. *"I went against my intuition, I had expectations he would look after me, I didn't want to take responsibility for myself!"* This enables us to start dissolving retained negative energy, opening up more space for different perspectives to emerge.

This questioning and awareness puts you in the driver's seat where you can change the things you did, rather than stay stuck and want him/her to change before you can. No one can make us feel any particular way, unless we let them. It's time to take your power back.

When we become more wholesomely aligned emotionally, mentally, physically, and spiritually, we find our sense of worth and realize we are all responsible for driving our lives!

In the early 1970s, American Psychologist Martin Seligman conducted experiments on dogs that led to the concept of learned helplessness.

'When people believe that their actions have no effect, they become passive. They learn helplessness instead of change.' – Martin Seligman

Can a Bed Make the Difference?

I'd been regularly working with this person for over a year supporting their process of 'letting go' and taking charge to open up to life again after the end of a long relationship.

Each step taken would end up in a few more forward, and at times some backward stumbles. With patient persistence they finally took their leap of faith and when I read this message they emailed me, it made everything I do worthwhile!

While I read the words I also felt a familiar vibration or frequency behind them – in some way, it related as much to what they were not saying, as much as what they actually verbally shared. The silence between the notes, as it were.

Maybe this simple, yet powerful message was for me, or maybe you, or maybe all of us?

'Hi Jilly,

Thank you for your session today. I got back in my garden with a new perspective. I'm not very good at saying how I feel – as you know.

When I was about to go to bed after rearranging my house with a bit of Feng Shui, I started thinking... I've been on my own for around 12 years now and realized I wasn't open to a new relationship...And I'm ok with that. However after today's session I'm sensing maybe I'm ready now?

Hence when I was getting into bed which is against the wall with no room for anyone else... it made me reflect for a moment, while I'm happy to have my own space, I think it's time to move my bed off the wall so there is space for someone else to come into my life.

I find it difficult to communicate my emotions and inner thoughts that's why I have written this email to express them to you.

Thank you for making me think and feel about all my possibilities and help me step into the driver's seat of my life!'

When you take responsibility to create your life, the pathway forward opens for you, even if the final destination looks beyond reach. Keep moving forward and what is meant to be for you will unfold in its own perfect time.

Never give up! Maybe we are all on the edge of a collective breakthrough, a shift in reality like the 'Hundredth Monkey Effect.'

One person breaks through, then another, and before long, suddenly the whole world embarks on a new era of change!

"Many of life's failures are people who did not realize how close they were to success when they gave up."
— Thomas Edison

 *Gateway Two*

Driver's Seat Exercises

1. Personal Power Inventory

Purpose: *Identify areas where you are already taking responsibility and others needing growth. Draw two columns on a page: "Where I Take Responsibility" and "Where I Don't Take Responsibility"*

* List situations, habits, or relationships under each column honestly.

* Reflect: What patterns do you see? What small step can you take today to shift from giving power away to owning it?

2. The Driver's Seat Visualization

Purpose: *Embody the feeling of being fully responsible for your life.*

* Close your eyes and imagine yourself sitting in the driver's seat of a car.

* Feel the steering wheel of life in your hands, the seat supporting you, and your feet on the pedals.

* Tune into your heart resonance and visualize the direction of your energy flow and let yourself go there.

* Notice any fears or doubts that arise and gently bring your focus back to the power of your heart and let them pass as if they were clouds.

* Open your eyes and write down insights or intentions from this visualization.

3. Choose Your Next Step

Purpose: *Practice gentle, conscious ownership by tuning in and choosing one clear, small step forward.*

* Sit quietly and take three deep breaths to settle your mind and body.

* Think about one area of your life where you feel stuck or out of control.

* Ask yourself: *What is one small, kind action I can take right now that would help me move forward?*

* Listen quietly for the answer? It might be simple, like making a phone call, saying no, or taking a walk in nature. Don't filter it. Don't look for a 'better suggestion' – trust your inner voice.

* Write down this next step and commit to doing it within the day.

* After completing it, pause and notice how it feels to *choose* your path and take responsible action towards making it happen.

4. Become Aware of Language Energetics

Purpose: *Transform victim mindset into empowered ownership.*

* Write about a recent challenging situation where you felt like a victim. e.g. *"I got fired and it wasn't my fault!"*

* Now rewrite the story from the perspective of; *"I am in the driver's seat"* e.g. *"I probably was bored with the job and not putting in 100%. Maybe they did me a favor as I do need to change my attitude!"*

* Focus on what you can control, what you learned, and how you can take empowered action moving forward e.g. *"When I get bored I need to take responsibility to change things so I can stay bright and engaged in whatever I'm doing, OR give my best to the situation and decide to leave as the job is not for me, rather than leave from letting it deteriorate to being fired!"*

5. Daily Choice Check-In

Purpose: *Practice conscious decision making to reinforce self-responsibility. Each morning or evening, pause and consider one choice you made.*

Ask yourself:

* Did I choose this consciously or out of habit/fear? e.g. *"Did I say yes to cooking dinner yet again, when I really wanted to say no, it's your turn?"* That was from fear.

* How did this choice serve my highest good? e.g. *"It didn't, it keeps the same pattern in place and builds resentment in me!"*

* Did blaming others affect my decision? *e.g. "I do blame my husband for never offering to cook dinner, so I never ask him, so yes, it does affect my decision!"*

* What if you changed your judgments and became curious about this situation? e.g. *"What if I talked to him about what he thinks about cooking dinner once a week and let him know this would mean a lot to me and make our family time more enjoyable?"*

Write in your journal how you feel after doing these exercises as it gives a sense of where you are now, and that anything can change in the next moment.

"We do not 'come into'
this world; we come out of it,
as leaves from a tree."

Alan Watts

Natural Connection

Symbiosis Of All Living Things

 *Big Picture*

We often see ourselves as flesh and bone, yet beneath the surface of our physical form, we are, at our core, energy in motion.

Every cell and atom in our body is made up of particles, electrons, protons and neutrons constantly moving and vibrating. The quantum field isn't some 'out there' concept, it's right here within us, pulsing with every heartbeat. We are living expressions of energy in physical form.

Long before concrete and clocks, we lived in rhythm with Earth and her celestial bodies. We honored them, not as distant objects, but as family. We danced under full moons, planted according to the lunar cycles, rose with the sun and offered gratitude to the stars.

But what if Mother Earth was the jewel in the crown of our solar system and she had fallen out of universal alignment because of our disharmony?

Over time we started to forget to value, listen, nurture and care for her, instead we mined her as if she was a commodity to be taken for granted and her resources endlessly used for our personal gain.

If we stopped and listened for a moment we might hear her whisper, whether through birdsong, a tree rustle, a water splash, or even the warmth of our breath. Pause. We can feel her presence consciously or unconsciously, in every cell. Nature holds the 'forever background' frequency while our human story commands our foreground presence and attention.

When we sense this greater connection and attune our frequency with nature's energy, she becomes responsive to us.

 This has been scientifically proven and wonderfully espoused in Lynne McTaggart's best-selling book *The Field: The Quest for the Secret Force of the Universe* published in 2003. Lynne shares numerous experiments carried out under strict scientific protocols to discover a connected living universe where human consciousness plays a central role.

What if Mother Nature was waking us up through the increase in volcanic eruptions, floods, wildfire, drought and winds as she endeavors to heal herself, and restore cosmic symbiosis.

She is holding a mirror up to humanity and asking each of us; *"Where are you angry and erupting inside? Where have you become rigid and flooded with ambition or dry with resentment? Where are you out of rhythm with yourself, others and your environment?"*

We are not here to fix ourselves or the planet, we are here to remember our true nature of oneness with all life exists in the quantum field of unconditional love where everything is connected. Once we understand that we know – hurt one, and we hurt all!

When we begin to value the purity of our energy and demonstrate this through our thoughts, choices, and actions, we naturally extend that vibration outwards, to the water, land, air, and stars, remembering life is sacred and all actions affect the whole.

It's about flowing with life, not fighting it! Any fight we carry externally will relate to the internal fight we have between head and heart – it is time to stop the fight, and come home to a truer self!

Personal Experience

Mountain Awakening

When I moved from the fast-paced rhythm of Sydney to a 20-acre farm nestled at the base of Mount Cooroy in Eumundi after my marriage ended, I wasn't just relocating, I was redefining who I was. It was the beginning of a new chapter and a chance to explore what I knew about security and identity.

I wanted to be brave, to stand strong in my new single life, however, under the quiet canopy of starlit skies and ancient trees, I felt exposed, like a visitor in someone else's world. The beauty was confronting. The silence and aloneness, overwhelming!

On my second night, lying in my four-poster bed gazing out the window at the mountain glowing silver under the moonlight, I was drifting into sleep when *thud, thud, thud,* I heard heavy pounding on the verandah which jolted me awake. Fear surged through me as I froze. I was in the middle of nowhere and my mind filled with terrifying thoughts of who (or what) was going to attack me!

In a flurry of adrenaline, I commando-rolled off the bed and crawled toward the sound, hiding behind furniture so I could spot the intruder before they saw me. Heart pounding in rhythm with the mysterious thuds, I waited, praying I would survive. Should I rush for a weapon – the kitchen knife perhaps? I reconciled that the element of surprise might be more advantageous than giving away my position. As it happened, like so often in life, I needn't have worried,

ENERGY MATTERS!

for it was not a hostile man nor a genuine threat; it was a giant kangaroo, curious, playful, simply welcoming me to his land.

I cried with relief, then laughed aloud! I wasn't being invaded; *I* was the intruder.

That night changed something, I began to understand the land didn't belong to me, I belonged to it. I was now part of something older, something intelligent and alive. As the weeks passed, I found myself living among creatures that didn't ask for permission to exist, including possums, rabbits, rats, pythons, birds, slugs, and snails, the latter two feasting on my veggie patch as if it was a gift. I stopped resisting, and started listening.

Mount Cooroy became my silent witness. A presence so ancient, I often felt it holding me like an invisible parent, giving energetic reassurance: *"You're safe here. You're not alone."* And every night, as the stars communed with the mountaintop, I felt something internal rise to meet them. It was as if they were whispering universal truths I had always known, but forgotten.

We are not separate from nature. We *are* nature!

 **Patterns**

* Disconnected from self by clinging to familiar roles, relationships, and environments

* Avoided fear by suppressing rather than exploring, stuck in old emotional loops

* Trying to control my surroundings, naively believing I owned or needed to manage everything.

* Prioritized busyness and distraction to avoid discomfort in stillness

* Overlooked deeper intelligence of life, dismissing the unseen and focusing on the proven and tangible

 *Effects*

* Living in the need to be in control, created constant tension and anxiety which separated my head and heart

* Prioritizing safety over natural experiences stopped me from really enjoying it

* Being rigid, inflexible and caught in overthinking, made me non-adaptive

* Trying to control fear rather than working through it, kept me superficial

* Not allowing vulnerability made me unrealistic

 *Professional Experience*

Cost of Separation

What I came to understand personally is exactly what I now see playing out professionally with many clients, the painful illusion of separation.

We have been taught to live as physical, logical human beings, cut off from the unseen intelligence that connects all of life. Our dominant culture told us there were five senses, and we believed it, however quantum physics has now proven we have infinite ways of perceiving, sensing, and knowing.

So when we feel discomfort, emotionally, mentally or

energetically, we automatically shut down those signals and default to control and mistake mental mastery for power. Not only are we controlling ourselves, but we are also endeavoring to control others, and our environment.

While this is how we have been conditioned, we need to appreciate that nothing has been lost; it's just been covered over. When we start to unwind from the old paradigm of separation by listening to a greater internal depth, we reclaim our innate sensitivity and become present, real, and effective by being harmonically in tune with our whole self.

It helps to rise above our challenges and take a 'bird's eye view' of life. This encourages our flexibility to understand different perspectives and see how the dots connect.

The willingness to move into this expanded view breaks through our fixed mindset patterns and enables greater awareness and understanding of self and others. This shift gives birth to clarity and an increased sense of freedom as our inflexibility gives way, and a whole new world reveals itself.

When we stop trying to control life and start attuning to it, we return to the flow of symbiosis. We shift from the mind's fears and limitations to the infinite flow of our sovereign heart resonance.

Abundance Web

A client shared her ponderings after a particularly deep session around manifestation.

As I was driving in peak hour traffic to my osteopath, a word flashed through my mind – 'gentleness'.

I could hear car horns, see frustrated faces mouthing expletives and generally marveled at how many of us get into our own angry bubble, trying to get work or appointments. It made me ponder the harsh inner and outer world we live in at times.

I put my indicator on to change lanes and checked my outside rear vision mirror. As I did so, I noticed a spider web on it.

For a moment I observed the delicateness of the web and how fragile and soft it looked, at the same time being robust and strong enough to hold firm to the mirror as it rode alongside me.

Do we tune in daily to that gentle, vulnerable place within us all, or does our mind completely control us and make life seem hard and success-focused?

What stops us from feeling our natural gentleness and vulnerability?

Is it our perceived needs and ego that drives us to achieve goals? Whether a professional athlete, banker, teacher, cleaner, nurse, or police officer, what motivates us?

If the focus is on money, can we lose ourselves in that quest?

We could unknowingly be in an automatic loop of chasing money whereby we start to value it beyond self and others and make it our priority.

*We could be totally unaware of how laser focused on finances we have become. The mind is 'booby trapped' to control us to believe **the only way we can be free is to have financial and physical security.***

Money is a piece of paper with a number on it that we physically exchange. Real value and self-worth comes from the exchange of our heart resonance energy which is priceless.

We have all contributed to creating a physical collective that totally relies upon money. It's not that we can't have a lot of money, it's the myopic importance we place on it that is the problem.

What if instead of money we replaced the word with 'love'? Do we share our love or keep it to ourselves to accumulate, so we can have as much as possible to spend on buying something or someone, so we can 'own' it, or them?

We are now living in a time where money is controlling the world. Maybe if each of us took it off the top of our own pile, it would dismantle the harsh world-wide money web and through being vulnerable and dismantling our own illusion, we'd find the wealth of our true worth?

I hope so!

B. Smith – Brisbane, Queensland

Natural Connection Exercises

Each exercise is designed to move you from disconnection to reconnection — with nature, energy, and your own inner rhythm.

1. Earth Listening

Purpose: *Reawaken the innate ability to sense and communicate with nature.*

* Go to a natural setting — a park, beach, forest, garden, or even a balcony with plants.

* Sit in silence for 10–20 minutes with the intention of *listening* rather than observing.

* Ask silently; *"What do you want me to know?"*

* Drop into your body and notice any sensations, images, emotions, or 'downloads' that arise.

* Record what you received in your journal – no editing, just raw communication. Let the words flow onto the page.

2. Elemental Mirror Mapping

Purpose: *Explore the reflection between your emotional state and nature's elements.*

Draw a page divided into four quadrants. Label them:
Fire – Water – Earth – Air

Now reflect: Write intuitively in each quadrant.

* *"Where in me is anger, passion, or burnout?"* (Fire)

* *"Where am I flooded with emotion or needing to flow?"* *(Water)*

* *"Where am I overly grounded or rigid?"* (Earth)

* *"Where am I scattered, flighty, or overthinking?"* (Air)

Now ask: *"What message is nature reflecting to me right now through this element?"*

3. From Linear to Spiral Time

Purpose: *Shift perception from productivity-focused time to rhythmic, soul-led time.*

For one day live in quantum 'spiral time', being present and conscious of unseen energy.

* No clocks, no checking the time.

* Let your body guide when to eat, rest, create, or connect.

* When you are in action, do it with complete presence. Stirring tea, brushing hair, walking, writing, even scrolling. Engage your focus into present time. Be truly mindful of all you do.

Write down your experience: *"How did this slower, cyclical rhythm affect my nervous system, my choices, and my sense of self?"*

4. Celestial Connection Practice

Purpose: *Rebuild conscious relationship with the cosmos — the sun, moon, ocean and stars.*

* At dawn or dusk, step outside and consciously greet the sky.

* Speak aloud or whisper, for example,

"I remember you. Thank you for your light, your rhythm, your presence."

★ Sit or lie under the sky (sunlight or starlight) for 10 minutes and observe the beauty, allowing your breath to slow and match the vastness.

Bonus: Begin tracking the moon cycle. The eight moon cycles are:

1. New Moon (plant intentions)

2. Waxing Crescent (nurture ideas)

3. First Quarter (take action)

4. Waxing Gibbous (refine and adjust)

5. Full Moon (release and celebrate)

6. Waning Gibbous (reflect and share)

7. Last Quarter (let go and forgive)

8. Waning Crescent (rest and restore)

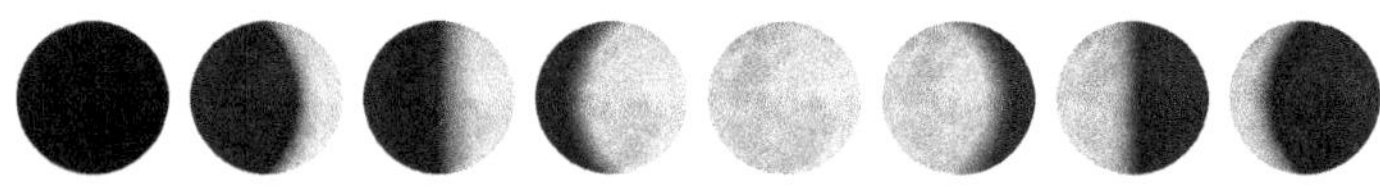

Check out the current phase of the moon and choose one intention to align with that movement. E.g. Waning Gibbous, time to reflect on my life and discover what needs to happen for me to move effortlessly forward!

5. Belonging to Nature

Purpose: *Move from ownership to belonging to shift the narrative of separation.*

* Stand barefoot on the earth, place your hands on a tree, eyes closed and feel the vibration from the tree's roots through to your hands, while giving your energy and acknowledgment. (Giving and Receiving Flow)

* Acknowledge your sacred relationship as you breathe and listen.

* Notice the subtle shifts in energy or emotion as you commune with nature.

Write in your journal how you felt after doing the Natural Connection exercises and do so from your feeling and emotions, not your thoughts.

When you change
the way you look at things,
the things you look at change.

Wayne Dyer

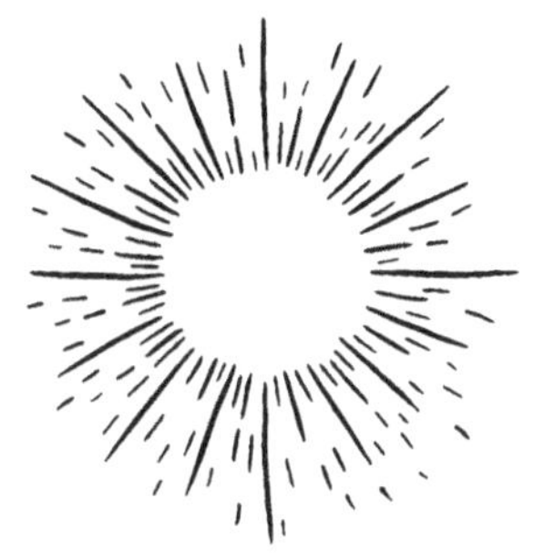

Untrue Belief Systems

Dissolving Old Restrictive Patterns

 *Big Picture*

Imagine waking up one day and realizing we had been living inside a giant belief system, almost like a movie set, without knowing. From birth we are handed the script of what to believe, how to behave and what success looks like.

Our world is then created by humanity's collective belief patterns, where thoughts have formed actions, and actions have become words recorded as 'truths'. Yet these inherited 'truths' have subtly limited us from realizing the boundless possibilities that exist beyond them.

Everyone forms their own interpretation, purely based on how much they need to belong to the group, or alternatively, how free and authentic they individually want to be.

We are energy and naturally flow in symbiosis with all living things, so when fixed beliefs are conditioned into our mind, they form barriers to expansion and our ability to adapt to our ever-changing world.

Our mind blocks our capacity to flow, and throws us into a black-and-white reality where logic is used against love and it becomes more important to gain, rather than give. The chance of loss raises our fears, spurring us on to fight harder, to build stronger internal resistance, to cling to things, and for the intellect to block the heart's resonance.

These belief patterns can be influenced by:

* **Race**, with its painful history of division

* **Ethnicity and culture**, woven into us before we can even speak

* **Class and gender roles**, scripting from others around our value and voice

* **Religion and nationhood**, defining what we should believe or defend

* **Family dynamics**, often passed down unconsciously like heirlooms of pain or pride

Some may say the Bible, or similar religious tomes, creates a set of beliefs, and corresponding stories, to give us a reference point of what it means to be a human being living on earth at any particular time.

For instance; 'An eye for an eye' found in the Old Testament of the Bible (Exodus 21:24), states that retaliation is justified. However, in the New Testament, Jesus moved from justice to mercy, non-retaliation and transformation over conflict. This higher belief shifts from protecting fairness, to breaking the cycle of harm altogether.

It is only by turning inwards, by meeting the parts of us we've hidden, or dismissed, that we begin to liberate ourselves from inherited restriction. When we shine light on old wounds and dissolve our coping behaviors, we begin to emerge, present, powerful and wholesome.

When we get upset about someone or something, we have unknowingly touched our inner fear as we feel some kind of attack. Someone has a different belief system to ours and because we think our system is the best, our mind fights against others who would rock the boat and disturb our secure world. Rather than addressing our discomfort, we blame and try to change the other person.

This blame encourages us to divide into tribes, territories, countries, and erect boundaries to assert the final separation. To keep these beliefs in place, we make others our enemy, and chose to fight them to gain more power, as greed and money drive us forward.

It also encourages acquisition and ownership, not sharing, and abandoning the notion of common unity for the greater good. We ended up in a linear world, heads full of limitations, asserted restrictive thoughts, and egocentric behaviors with matching actions and results.

Group-mind beliefs have developed into fixed rules humanity is now rebelling against, as they are based on control and restriction, to erode our freedom of spirit. We are currently experiencing the breakdown of all systems:

* **Political Systems** – collapse of public trust in governments, electoral processes and international bodies and leaders

* **Social Systems** – breakdown of traditional social contracts, institutional loyalty, lifelong careers

* **Gender Systems** – questioning binary gender definitions and expansion into fluid identity frameworks

* **Health Systems** – distrust in mainstream medical systems and pharmaceutical companies

* **Education Systems** – distrust of early learning care and erosion of belief in formal learning institutions

* **Environmental Systems** – exposure of false environmental solutions to mask ongoing planetary harm

* **Economic Systems** – erosion of trust in banking, inflation, debt cycles, scams, and currency instability

* **Legal Systems** – systemic bias, outdated laws of race, class, gender and economic status

* **Religious Systems** – decline of organized religious influence with exposure of hidden agendas

* **News Media Systems** – collapse of mainstream media through bias, propaganda, manipulation and social media.

* **Technology Systems** – pushback against big tech monopolies and ownership, privacy and AI.

* **Agriculture Systems** – questioning unethical farming, regeneration, pesticides and additives

* **Family Relationship Systems** – structural change beyond tradition, marriage, parenting, caregiving and aged care

* **Social/Celebrity Media Systems** – explosion of distrust with millions of influencers chasing fame, celebrity mistrust and false AI creations

The source of these control systems is being questioned, as they are rooted in untruths and hidden agendas to advance the few, to the detriment of the greater good of humanity. When we remember we are one group of people, on one planet, and we align with our original integrity, our resulting actions make it **impossible** to harm another.

We see animals, the Earth, and each other, not as separate, but as extensions of ourselves. Our core seed is unconditional love, free from conditions, beliefs, or imposed rules. In that space, infinite abundance is our natural state.

Individually and collectively we are at a crossroads point with humanity dividing into two realities, those willing to let to let go and travel into the unknown potential, and those who choose to stay safe, secure in the established rules. We will all experience the results of our choice.

Key Learning: *We are caught in untrue beliefs that restrict our potential.*

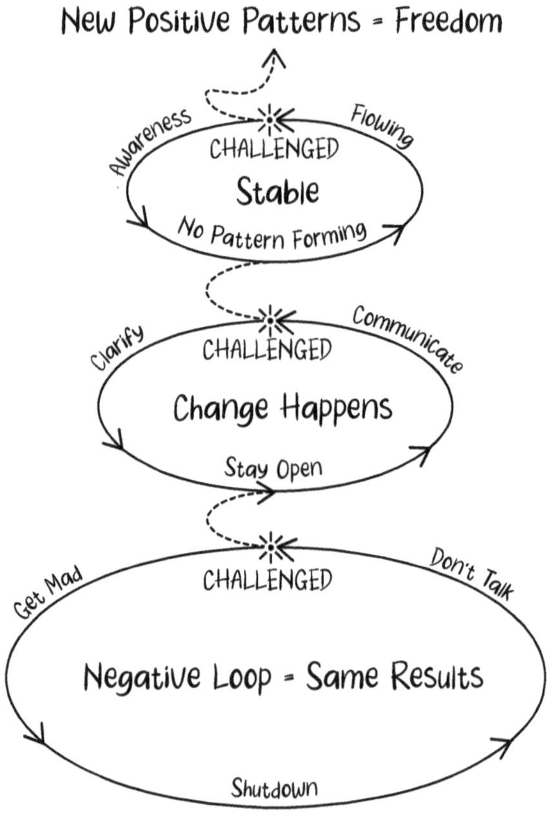

We get caught in belief loops and keep getting the same results e.g. "When challenged, I get mad, I shutdown, I don't talk" and nothing changes until I become aware this doesn't work any more. When we feel the pattern of our 'new' awareness we release the negative energy and rise into a more authentic loop until we free ourselves from loops all together, as we align with our integrity.

 *'Believing in negative thoughts is the single greatest obstruction to success!'* – Charles F. Glassman – American Physician and Author of Brain Drain

 ***Personal Experience***

The Invisible

When I was a child, I used to wake up crying in the middle of the night, terrified my mum was going to die. She was healthy, living right there in the house, but the fear was so strong it felt real. I'd go to her room and crawl into her arms, and she would hold me until I fell asleep. That fear stayed with me for years, quiet, unspoken, until she eventually passed away at 65.

Some part of me always felt responsible for her, especially spiritually. I could sense when she was sad or struggling. She'd cry sometimes, not in front of everyone, but I saw it. She had a difficult childhood and just wanted to create a kind and loving family that was hers.

My dad was a compassionate and supportive husband, but I sensed he was unable to emotionally give her what she really needed. She had healing to do that no one else could do for her. And he too, had his own wounds, being the middle child growing up in a family where his older professional athlete brother got most of the praise.

They were carrying their childhood emotional restrictions that formed beliefs around 'not being good enough or similar'. I was carrying a belief that somehow I was responsible for their happiness and lost myself in being a 'pleaser' to seek validation.

I may have come into this world with a belief, or created it from an early age, that it was my fault if people were not happy, so I tried to make others happy which ended up being total control and inauthenticity. It's a form of victim hood where we are always trying to help others so we will be loved and valued rather than finding the value in our natural selves and supporting others to do the same, as no-one is a victim to life.

It's not about age or size, as our spirit is ageless, and we have already chosen our particular mission.

That's why it is important as parents to communicate honestly to our children even when we are having difficulties so they understand we are moving through our emotions and feelings so they can dissolve. Just like a cloud passing by in the sky. Children then become aware they can do the same and don't have to hide their emotions and feelings which form negative beliefs.

Untrue beliefs cause separation when all we **really want** is to come together in the truth of love within ourselves and with others.

 *Patterns*

* Losing self in what others wanted me to be.

* Gaining love by being a 'good girl/partner'.

* Manipulation of love by being covert with thoughts and actions.

* Putting attention on others to divert pressure from self.

 *Effects*

* ⭑ Unconsciously separated my head and heart to cope.

* ⭑ Suppressed my genuine emotions and feelings, and became numb, delusional and inauthentic.

* ⭑ Highly critical of self, I created irrational thoughts and actions.

* ⭑ Always trying hard to deliver what others wanted, and often emotionally disappointed in self, no matter how well I did.

 *Professional Experience*

Vulnerability Dissolves Barriers

I'm often shocked at how cruel and harsh we are with ourselves in not acknowledging our vulnerability when we are falling apart. Just scratch the surface through the 'feeling' area and a protective fight comes up to repel anyone who touches the 'strength' of ego or the 'weakness' of victimhood, as both are different sides of the same coin. Rather than asking for help or support we push our upset down and pretend we are okay.

This is understandable, as few of us have known how to be true to ourselves emotionally, mentally, physically, and spiritually and, without that reference point, the mind is in charge. Its job is to hold authority by being a harsh inner critic, highlighting our faults and causing us to doubt our abilities.

Our untrue beliefs hold this network together and inhibit awareness of the power we have given to words that have formed beliefs and then made them seem true. All that has happened is we experienced something we didn't understand, felt hurt and set a belief up to protect ourselves e.g. *"Don't be vulnerable as you'll get hurt!"* then got on with our lives trying not to be vulnerable.

It's not so much about the experience, it's how uncomfortable it made us feel, and we locked in our belief in order to never to feel that way again. Whenever that similar feeling is triggered, the belief pops up to defend itself. The only way to dissolve these untrue mindsets is to feel and release the held energy.

I recently touched this area in a middle-aged businessman and experienced directly his instinct to fight rather than reveal any vulnerability. Out came the boardroom ego and he let rip with a hurtful tirade making it personal to me hoping to shut me down.

I wasn't having a bar of his antics! I knew he adhered to the belief; *"The best form of defense is attack!"* I held his 'beingness' while I talked to his mindset behavior and said; *"You are selfish and stuck on yourself – whatever you do, there is always an agenda for you to win. You might win in business with those tactics however you can't control your estranged children's love and that's what's upsetting you, not me! You're here now because you're ready to change that. The fight is not with me, it's with yourself!"*

His chest deflated and all of a sudden, as his fight energy relinquished, tears rolled down his face. *"I don't know any other way!"* he lamented. I gently replied, *"You, do, it's just been covered over and protected for a long time. Today you've started to let go of your fight and a whole new way forward will reveal itself."*

Most of us have some kind of fight in us between our head and heart, where we have lost trust and have found comfort in simply feeling safe. This separation from self-belief has formed a collective system where human beings have become less potent, a little like the photocopier mentioned in an earlier chapter, when the original has been copied, then recopied over and over, until the image has become so distorted, the original version is virtually indiscernible.

Our faded memory of our true self has driven us to become more controlled, and physically entrenched in systems, as we lock into untruths, which make us even more distorted.

If anyone disagrees with the 'norm' they are labeled rebellious, conspiracy theorists or just dismissed as 'crazy' and are marginalized by society which separates human beings into 'warrior' groups and keeps everyone controlled and unaware, through fixed viewpoints.

It is not from the outside that we see whom we need to separate from, it's by looking inside to discover our heart disconnection. When our mind is overactive our thoughts and feelings are controlled, and in turn, we become controlling of others to get what we 'think' we want, and are often willing to fight for it.

Life isn't about what we 'want' as that is limited thinking. Sure, we can want our lives to look a certain way, however when they don't, how do we address that? By looking at every experience as an opportunity or lesson to grow, life begins to flow and guides us forward to where we are meant to be. Many of us have settled physically for far less than the endless possibilities available! Some of us have spent our lives blocking awesome alternatives because our controlling, limited thoughts drove us to what we 'wanted'.

Our birthright is endless freedom outside all beliefs and is ours to have at any time we choose, it's infinite and can never be lost, only if we get lost!

Buried Treasure Of You!

I worked with a young man recently, and was able to feel where he was holding on to control and not being his true self. He was happy for me to share this recall of his session with you.

He could feel how he had created a "fake" version of himself and was upset that people treated him that way, rather than who he truly was.

I felt deeply connected to his energy as he allowed himself to travel through his emotions. It was truly astonishing how heartfelt he was. His words were like arrows penetrating my heart.

Even though I was the therapist, his energy enabled a wound healing in me, and vice versa. Through the energetic duplication of his hurts and upsets, I was able to feel and understand the buried treasure hidden under untrue beliefs for lifetimes.

These deeper feelings are often unknown territory until we let ourselves connect with them and have the courage to communicate in a safe space with another.

We talk about 'knowing our feelings', but often this is intellectual and similar to cutting the tops off weeds, the same emotions grow again if we don't remove the roots. It is in the depth of being able to feel the 'root cause' of our wounds that releases the untruths and this shift immediately creates lasting, positive, emotional change.

Once he broke through the ego's resistance, he started to travel into unknown territory and through authentic communication, was able to share with me his deepest fears, and how he had unknowingly manipulated himself to cope by creating a fake persona. He believed this made him more acceptable to others, particularly in relationships!

I actively listened as the liquid gold of hurt and disillusionment around love released, going beyond the mind's perception of 'not good enough' to where the bright, sovereign 'being' emerged, like a new person!

It was a game changer for him, and me!

As he was leaving, he skipped out of the room with renewed energy, and glancing back over his shoulder, I caught the glint in his eye, knowing from that moment, he was free to be his true self.

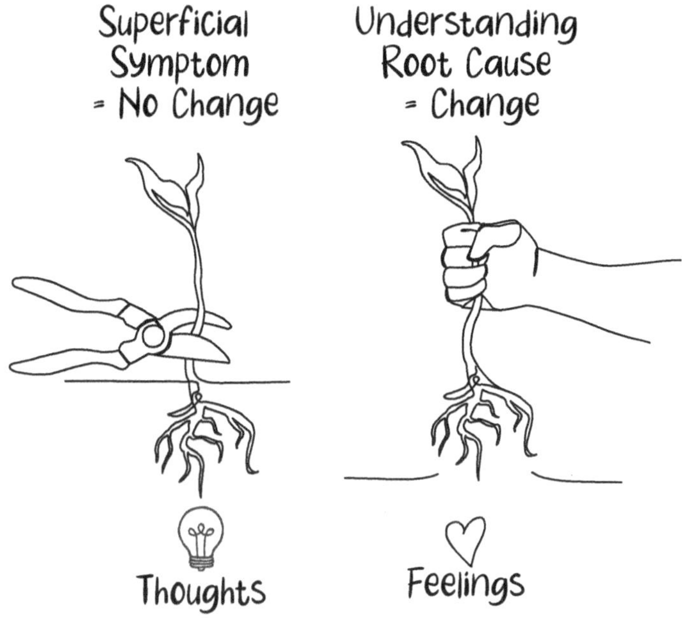

Key Learning: *Intellectual knowing of behavior cuts the 'weed' where it is seen and attends only to the symptom, and will grow again.* **Heartfelt feeling dissolves the behavior at the root cause,** *and the energy releases through understanding and awareness where the weed can no longer grow.*

 *Gateway Four*

Untrue Belief Systems Exercises

Purpose: *Transform fixed mindsets into the freedom of creation!*

* Write about a recent challenge where you had a fixed belief you couldn't change. e.g. *"I knew it was wrong about what I was saying but I didn't want to back down."*

* Tune in to any part you may have played in the situation developing. e.g. *"I feel I have to have the answers, so I assert I have them rather than being honest and asking what another thinks."*

* Now rewrite the story from a different perspective to experience a new result.

* Focus on what you became aware of, what you learned, and how you can take empowered action moving forward.

Daily Choice Check-In

Purpose: *Practice conscious decision-making to reinforce self-responsibility.*

* For one day you are going to hop in your magical helicopter and observe your life. As you hover above your physical story and experiences watch yourself tune in to your feelings, thoughts and actions while you are physically experiencing them. Also feel into other people and what is going on for them, beyond their physical story.

* Write down your experience of this exercise from your perspective and the perspective you observed in others.

* What were five keys you became aware of? e.g. *"I noticed I don't really listen, I'm always waiting to jump in and quickly say what I want to say."*

* Now put them into practice the following day. e.g. *"Today I will make the effort to listen more and talk less."*

* At the end of that day, write down your experience.

The Invisible Script

Purpose: *Awareness of beliefs and perspectives.*

* Find a quiet space where you can sit undisturbed for at least 15–20 minutes.
* Take three slow breaths and gently close your eyes.
* Imagine your life as though it were a stage play.

Visualize:

* The roles you have played
* The expectations placed upon you
* The beliefs you inherited from family, culture, religion, education or society
* The behaviors you learned in order to belong, survive or be accepted

Now ask yourself slowly:

* *Whose voice still lives in my mind?*
* *What beliefs have I accepted without questioning?*
* *What parts of myself have I hidden to fit in?*
* *Where do I seek approval instead of truth?*

Allow whatever arises to surface naturally.

"The best and most beautiful things in the world cannot be seen or even touched — they must be felt with the heart."

Helen Keller

Inner Senses

Listening to the Body's Wisdom

 *Big Picture*

Life begins to transform when we awaken to our true sensory capacity, not limited to five, but limitless as all are doorways into deeper understanding of the self.

How often do we pause long enough to notice our breath? If we did, how long could we stay present, clear minded and let our thoughts float by like clouds?

In the same way, when was the last time we truly listened to our body, not just when it aches or fails us, but when it is quietly sustaining our life, moment to moment?

Are we ever aware of our lungs expanding and contracting, our heart pulsing, our cells circulating and our bones holding us upright? Probably not, it just happens for us! Maybe it's time to thank our internal organs for the great job they are doing?

Too often we only notice the body when something goes wrong, when we resist, complain, feel unfairly treated and forget the constant miracle of everything going right in every second of our existence.

In moments of stress or difficulty, the mind quickly takes over and catastrophizes, criticizes, compares and fills us with endless 'what ifs'. One moment our mind undervalues us, telling us we are hopeless or not enough, the next it overvalues us, inflating us with superiority. Yet both are illusions of the same thing, the absence of genuine self-love.

The more we turn inward and sense beyond the noise, we begin to hear a deeper calling. We start to realize our external world mirrors our internal one.

For example, what we see on the surface of a tree is the trunk, leaves and branches, yet this is only part of the picture. The real life force flows underground, in the unseen root system, sustained by hidden networks that nourish its visible beauty.

The same is true for the health of our inner landscape as it is determined by the nurturing quality of our thoughts, emotions and energy. The external world is only a reflection to highlight where we are flowing and where we are depleting ourselves. With our focus outside ourselves, we disconnect from our inner guidance and become unnatural, blocked versions of self.

When we pay attention to the clues the body gives us, a tight chest, a heavy stomach, a wave of tingles, we are really listening to the language of the universe flowing through us. I'm sure you can relate when you hear someone singing a beautiful song and it sends goose-bumps through us as the external vibration meets our internal vibration.

This demonstrates the importance of looking after ourselves and being aware of what we put into our bodies, the relationships we engage with and the environments we place ourselves in.

Every choice ripples through our inner landscape and out again into the greater field. Caring for ourselves is not a small, private act, it's the symbiosis of life, and **it matters**.

 *'When you go to school, you learn to use logic and reason and to squash any quote-unquote 'magical thinking.' And yet it is an instinct—it's designed to save our lives.'* – Dr Emma Seppala, Psychologist, author of Time Magazine article, *The Science of Intuition—and How to Tune Into Your Own*

 **Personal Experience**

Wake Up Body

I was aware of looking after my health and thought I'd done a good job until my early fifties. It was then it became clear that I had not truly connected with my internal body. Like many of us, I ate healthily, exercised, had body work alignments and massages, along with kinesiology, flower essences, bio-resonance therapy, etc. I thought I knew plenty about the body's energy however, there was a gap with intellectually 'knowing', and heartfelt 'knowing' – where the inner connection was felt.

I still viewed 'health' as an external fix whereby I needed to find things on the outside, to address my health inside. It wasn't until I started to wake up and think, "What if my cells were originally healthy and they knew how to heal themselves, I only have to listen to what they need and be in tune with their voice?"

When I listened, I started making different choices, albeit subtle. I noticed my body changing over time. I would often have stomach aches from worrying and as we know, the gut holds our feelings, which is why some call it our 'second heart', hence 'gut instincts' or being 'gutted'. The connection between brain and gut is now universally recognized by nutritionists and healthcare practitioners.

Combine that with emotional sensitivity and I feel my health could have gone off track if I hadn't started to listen more deeply and make different decisions. Those choices were not intellectual and logically based, they came more from listening to what my body told me it needed. Everything I did I endeavored to do as naturally as possible so I could be in tune by listening to my intuition.

I became more aware of the negative effects of not eating organically, electro-magnetic radiation, technology affecting my cells, the purity of water, exposure to toxic materials, cleaners, pharmaceuticals, synthetic clothing and air-conditioning.

My energy levels lifted as a consequence of the healthy choices I made. No more aches or pains and life became more meaningful and connected. Now I am older, I feel and experience how beneficial those changes made years ago have been to my current health.

I'm not rigid, as that forms controlling energy and can restrict us having to have things a certain way to be okay. Our spirit is more powerful than any physical element and at times flexibility is required.

It's also important to change patterns of eating, exercising, drinking so our body doesn't become reliant on one way of being healthy – as different parts grow and change they may need attention.

Many people believe in psychosomatic illness, which is when we are not clearing the body of toxic emotional energy and it is pushed down and stored, rather than released. What happens is wherever we are susceptible in our body it will start communicating to us with headaches, heartaches, back aches or cellular dis-EASE to let us know attention is required.

I've personally experienced this when I would push emotions down thinking it was the only way to cope. I found it challenging to take ownership of all the hurt and upset I'd caused myself and others however it released my stuck emotional energy. Old coping mechanisms were naturally replaced by being vulnerable with my true feelings. This created real change and helped me return to emotional, mental, physical and spiritual wellbeing.

 ***Patterns***

* Pushing down uncomfortable emotions and feelings, believing they didn't matter.

* Presenting an attractive outside appearance to distract from inside turmoil.

* Believing having something wrong was bad, therefore it had to be hidden.

* Attending to symptoms of health rather than addressing the root cause.

* Not trusting intuition or gut instincts.

 *Effects*

* Mind control to avoid vulnerability, then blaming others for their same lack.

* Living inauthentically by being superficial, to cover over weaknesses.

* Caring and trusting others more than self, which caused loss of direction and blame.

* Believing I had it together created a false image of superficial self that confused me and others.

 *Professional Experience*

Beingness

As human beings, few of us tune in to the invisible 'being' part of ourselves, as we are conditioned to focus on the *visible* human, leaving our inner energetic world with little to no attention.

The only way to combine these fields is by being present and bringing attention to the moment, just as you are reading this book, at this very moment!

Everything is available in present time as it is our creation point and the field that connects our physical and metaphysical story into a greater truth.

To stabilize this inner presence we need to release the buried layers of negative thoughts primarily focused around survival and fears, particularly of dying as these traumas have been held for lifetimes and are ready to be released.

When our mind carries heavy internal burdens the weight can transfer to the body and our living becomes linear and labored as we logically work our way through life carrying this load.

Whatever we put our attention on is reinforced. It sets up matching operating patterns and actions that bring about the same results as we limit our potential to draw in new information to shift old, worn-out mind pathways.

When working with clients it is necessary to be present. My whole attention is on the human being as they unwind their negative mind thoughts and stories through heartfelt communication. As the old, heavy energy dissolves through awareness, it unties the knots of hurt, enabling their natural flow to return.

With this freedom a new higher vibrational pattern forms, aligning greater wholesomeness and ability to experience joy from a bigger picture.

It's a magical experience to witness someone carrying a lifetime of heavy burdens and to observe their dissolution and movement into sovereignty.

The River = Our Nature

Continue to flow through challenges
by going over, under, around
- not stuck on the riverbank!

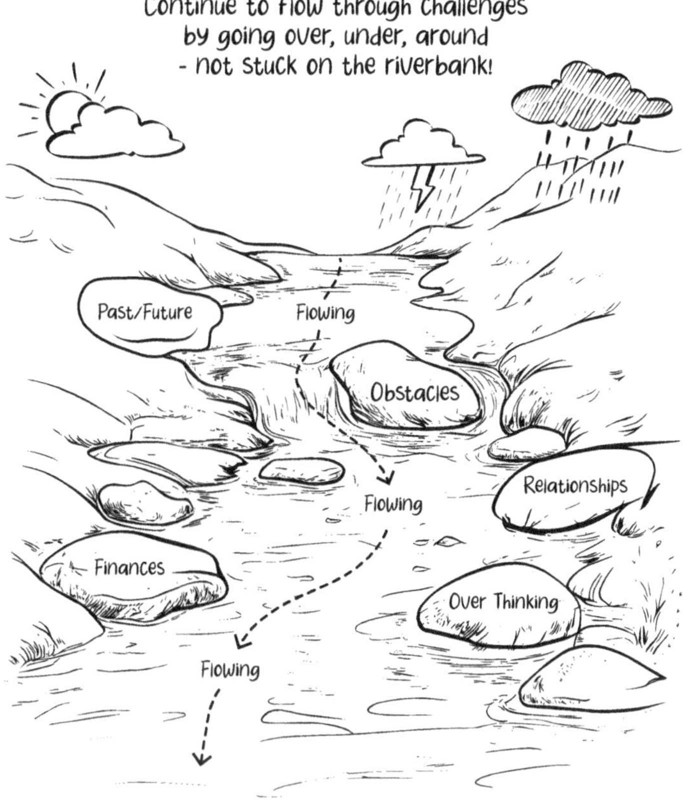

Key Learning: *Stay in **your natural flow and be guided by your inner knowing** through challenges rather than stuck on the riverbank of overthinking and stressful mind games. No matter the weather, the river continues to flow in the same direction and holds its innate nature of always being able to find its original source.*

 *Client Story*

I wrote this after working with a client and used the river as metaphor for their life.

The River – Ability to Go With the Flow

Lately, my life has felt like a river; I'm not quite sure where I'm heading, but for the first time, I'm okay with that.

It's as if I've connected to a natural flow within and have become the river. I›m staying with this movement and not letting my mind control anything. I'm finding it's taking me a different way than I expected. It's making me do uncomfortable things yet I'm going with it, not resisting, not fighting, not staying 'safe', just having new experiences.

As part of the ecosystem of life, flowing is our nature. When we stop flowing, we get stuck, caught on the riverbank, trapped in our head. That's when blame, harsh judgments and frustration start and we become victims, wanting others to change before we can move.

Our bodies are wise. Every cell vibrates with life when we're living in flow, when we're aligned, rested, nourished, and honest with ourselves. However, when we cling to old thoughts, fears, and habits, energy can't move freely. The body feels it, and demonstrates it to us in the form of headaches, backaches, skin flare-ups, heart strain – all signs we're out of sync. Out of the flow!

The real energetic shift begins when we stop trying to control everything through our mind and start curiously looking within to discover the unknown about ourselves.

When we open the door to flexibility instead of certainty... When we allow different perspectives, even when they're uncomfortable...

                    ENERGY MATTERS!

When we stop clinging to the old stories and behaviors to avoid feeling, then we start to move more freely.

Yesterday, I had a wellness session with a client and planned to work through some staff issues. When we connected on Zoom, she told me her mum wasn't well.

In that moment, everything changed. I let go of the agenda. I dropped into presence. I listened. And that simple act took us somewhere much deeper.

Together, we gently explored her emotions, layer by layer. She spoke of fear, grief and frustration. She then hit a wall and said, "I don't want to go any further."

I reassured her: "That's just your mind trying to protect you. Your heart knows how to do this. You've been here before, this time you're ready to go further."

And she did.

She cried as she cracked open. She said the thing she'd been avoiding out loud: "I'm afraid to feel how much I love her… because if she goes, I don't know how I'll survive it."

So instead, she'd kept herself safe by being practical, capable, and always busy. She gave love through doing, not feeling, to everyone.

What she didn't know was that her love didn't need to be earned. Her love was the power, the healing, the medicine, it was enough!

As she freed herself, there was great beauty, as she was also freeing her mother.

When we hold onto fear, we energetically bind the people we care about, too. When we let go, we unlock the space for everyone to expand and fresh possibilities to activate.

Real healing is not about "fixing" anything. As we become aware of our internal truth the controlling hidden untruths dissolve as the lesser frequency collapses.

By the end of our session, her energy had shifted. Her heart was gentle, open and powerful. There was nothing left to do, it was time for her to simply be.

If you're feeling stuck, overwhelmed, or unsure... maybe you're just paused on the riverbank, waiting to remember, you are the river.

 *Gateway Five*

Inner Senses Exercises

All these exercises and techniques help to understand, acknowledge and be grateful to the body as the vehicle that holds our life experiences.

There are four categories:

* **Everyday Tools** (Breathwork, Movement, Journaling, Sleep, Nature Walks, Nourishment, Environment)

* **Body-based Therapies** (Yoga, Acupuncture, EFT, Reiki etc.)

* **Emotional Healing Modalities** (Counseling, Life Coaching, Mentoring, Therapy)

* **Spiritual Connection** – (Meditation/Visualization/Stillness/Rituals)

Breathwork – Source of Life

We all lead busy lives so we have condensed these exercises into short sessions, so there are no excuses – at a minimum, aim for five times per week.

A very powerful, simple, and effective start to your morning! The **6-2-7-3 Breath**. It balances the nervous system, energizes the body and clears the mind. **(3 mins)**

1. Inhale gently through your nose for 6 seconds. (Let your belly rise and fill your lungs)

2. Hold for 2 seconds. (Just a short pause to absorb the oxygen)

3. Exhale slowly through your mouth for 7 seconds, (Release the stale air, tension and mind clutter) then hold for 3 breaths.

Movement – Body Reset

This sequence of movements will stretch tight muscles, align spine and joints, along with energizing the breath and circulation for stability, flexibility and longevity.

Awaken The Body – Arm Stretch (1 min)

1. Stand tall, feet hip-width apart and **inhale with arms lifted up overhead** and stretched out long.

2. Exhale while dropping the arms down, soften your shoulders.

3. Repeat 6-8 times with deep breaths (Opens lungs and wakes up circulation).

Spine Stretch (1 min)

1.   Get onto all fours on a good surface or mat.

2.   Inhale and arch spine, lift chest and tailbone (Cow Pose).

3.   Exhale and round spine, tucking your chin under (Cat Pose).

4.   Flow with your breath, slow and smooth (Aligns spine, massages organs, releases stiffness).

Refresh Nervous System (1 min)

1.   Stand, feet hip-width apart.

2.   Inhale as you raise your arms up, exhale and fold forward with soft knees.

3.   Roll up slowly to stand on the inhale.

Release Back Tension (1 min)

1.   Stand tall, arms out to the sides.

2.   Gently twist torso right and lift, letting arms swing loosely.

3.   Keep hips facing forward, just swing the top half of your body.

Hip & Leg Awakener (1 min)

1.   Step one leg back into a low lunge (hands on thighs or floor).

2.   Inhale and lift chest.

3.   Exhale, shift back into a gentle hamstring stretch.

Journaling

* Each morning before getting out of bed write how you feel in your journal.

* Reflect at the end of each week on your journal writings and feel what the overall flavor of the week was – write down your gains and your challenges.

* At end of the month reflect back and in one word, how would you sum up the month?

Sleep

* Keep a consistent schedule of going to bed and waking up for five days – let your natural body clock operate on the weekends.

* Create a wind-down routine by disconnecting from screens, dimming the lights, calming the body and thoughts with breathing.

* Optimize sleep environments by keeping bedroom cool, dark, quiet, and comfortable for your mind, body, and spirit to rest deeply.

* Limit stimulants and heavy meals and also avoid caffeine and alcohol 3-4 hours before bed.

* Manage stress and overthinking by using relaxation techniques such as meditation, journaling, gentle stretches, and breathing.

Nature Walking

* Notice how you sit, stand, and move.

* Good alignment frees energy flow, supports organ function, and affects mood.

* Poor posture often reflects mental or emotional contraction, so adjust physically to shift internally.

* When walking in nature be present and connect with the giving and receiving of Mother Earth. Observe the trees, water, birds, flowers, notice the energy coming from nature, and absorb it into every cell, then give it back through your acknowledgment and gratitude to nature.

* Stay very present when walking and if thoughts arise, let them come and go like clouds.

Fuel & Nourishment

* Eat more living, whole foods, especially pesticide-free vegetables and nuts.

* Drink plenty of pure, filtered water (8 glasses a day).

* Reduce refined carbs like white bread, pasta, and rice.

* Limit alcohol and drug use as it confines true aligned expansion.

* If using supplements make sure they are of high quality.

* Always check ingredients labeling, and stay away from chemicals where possible.

Environmental Energetics

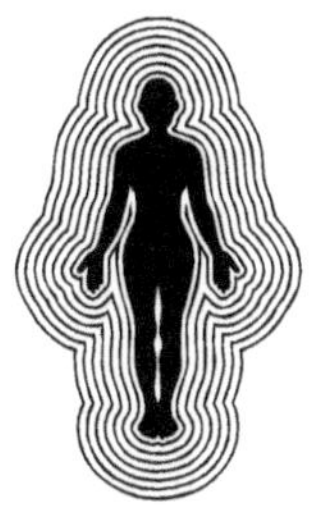

* Become aware of your body and where energy feels expansive or constricted.

* Keep EMR electronic devices out of bedroom and don't carry them on your body.

* Use gentle movement, stretching or breath work to release negative blockages.

* Notice environments, people, and activities that make you feel either energized or drained.

Emotional Healing Therapies

* Counselor/Life Coach/Mentor/ Therapist – find the mental health support needed to maintain wellbeing as it helps to gain outside perspectives from professionals who can shine a light on places that have been hidden and need healing.

* Self-help Books/Podcasts can support conscious awareness.

* Group Work – Finding like-hearted people interested in individual collective growth.

Body-Based Healing

* Bush Flower Essences – natural remedies that gently balance emotions and restore inner harmony.

* Bio-resonance Feedback Therapy – Uses energy frequencies to detect imbalances and supports natural body healing.

* Kinesiology – Muscle testing to identify stress patterns and restore your body's alignment.

* Acupuncture/Acupressure – Stimulates energy pathways to relieve tension and promote overall wellbeing.

* Reiki – Gentle energy practice that channels healing through the hands to rebalance the body.

* Osteopathy – Hands-on treatment that restores structure and movement to balance the body.

Spiritual Connection Practices

* Meditation – Cultivates inner calm and presence through focused awareness.

* Visualization – Uses the mind's imagery to create healing, clarity and relaxation.

* Stillness – A conscious pause that connects with a deeper space within – often eyes are closed.

* Rituals – Intentional practices honoring transitions and meaning to life.

* Prayer – Heartfelt dialogue to deepen connection with the divine or higher self.

Write in your journal how you feel about your health and rate yourself out of ten, then use this as your baseline for improvement.

"Happiness is when what you think, what you say, and what you do are in harmony."

Mahatma Gandi

Communication

Effective Exchange Changes Everything

 *Big Picture*

Communication is more than words. It's an exchange of energy, an invisible current that creates harmony or separation between someone, or something. At its best, it manifests common union, a shared space where connection, understanding, and trust naturally grow.

Our very first communication begins not with another, but with ourselves. As babies we cry, not from learned words or social conditioning – it's from raw expression, need, truth, and life force we hold deep within.

This is our original source and as we grow, it colors how critical or compassionate we are with ourselves and others. When our inner dialogue is honest and aligned, our sharing carries this resonance and people hear and feel our words.

When the source of words is solely spoken from the mind they can feel cold, hollow or disconnected. They may be technically correct, however, they lack the ability to penetrate the heart and be remembered. When words have warmth and are true, they are received at a deeper level and are likely to be acted upon.

Every relationship, whether personal, professional, or intimate is built on communication. With each exchange we either strengthen the bond through building connection, or weaken it through separation. Sometimes we judge someone's words and filter them through our belief system, forming immediate opinions that can block us from receiving ***their*** message.

Flexibility and curiosity are key. For instance, if you don't understand or agree with what someone has said, you could say; ***"I'm not sure I understand, could you share that another way, as I genuinely want to connect***

with you?" Spoken with sincerity, this approach evokes trust and greater understanding.

This requires moving beyond ego where everything circles back to us. We need to be genuinely interested and attentive to the other person. Real communication begins in a shared field of respect, where two people work together to create a wholesome connection.

The way we communicate determines the quality of our relationships. If we stay light, sarcastic, or guarded, our connections will reflect that. If we bring honesty, vulnerability, and genuine care, those same qualities will echo back to us. Communication mirrors the energy and intention we bring to it.

Many people believe they need 'different' communication styles for work and home, however this belief often creates a false dichotomy within us. The truth is, we are the same human being wherever we go, no labels required. Whether speaking to a colleague, a partner, or a child, the most powerful words come from the same heartfelt source of trust, respect, and authenticity.

Even in high-stakes conversations, integrity wins. We all have inner radars that can detect when something feels 'off'. Our body talks, the gut tightens, our heart senses a lack of congruence and our intuition speaks to us softly; "It's not true!" These subtle unspoken signals are just as powerful as the spoken word, and when they don't align, we have a communication breakdown.

When we allow our heart intelligence to guide our words, something remarkable happens. Communication shifts from simply being an exchange of words and information to a meaningful sharing of a harmonious tune.

The other person hears and feels us, which creates space for new possibilities. Conversations become transformative, turning simple exchanges into opportunities for deeper relationships, collaboration, and that's when the magic happens!

Four people enter a room with a huge black and white ball, and only see what is in front of them. When asked over a loudspeaker, all believe they are 100% correct on what they see, yet all disagree with each other. It takes one person to be flexible and suggest a helicopter view, who will come? All but one travel into the bigger picture and they come together. The one person who believes they are 100% 'right', leaves the room believing everyone else wrong, highlighting their own inflexibility and control. Flexibility is the key.

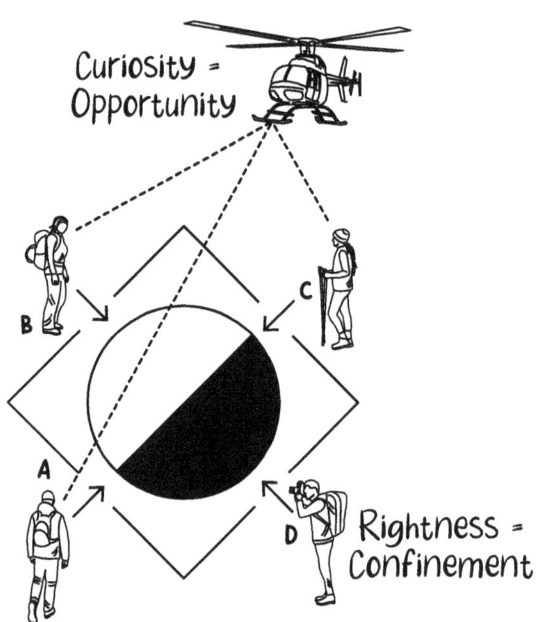

Key Learning: *Where is your energy coming from to communicate? Are you being right and inflexible or open with curiosity?*

Outcome of Learning: *Person 'D' continues to live their life in 'rightness', not prepared to be open to new possibilities, confined by their limited mind and missing out on the genuine opportunity to be connected. Conversely, persons A, B and C, come together into a new understanding where all are on the same page.*

'Inconsistencies between verbal and nonverbal cues can lead to confusion and reduce perceived sincerity and trustworthiness.' – Research on the Role of Consistency in Verbal and Nonverbal Communication (European Research Studies Journal Volume XXVII, Issue 3, 2024)

 *Personal Experience*

The Unheard Communication

Communication comes in countless forms and I'm sharing a deeper form of personal communication, beyond language, to speak to you through my feelings.

I only had one child, though my heart always wanted more.

Jack came into my life at a time when everything felt new; marriage, motherhood and the overwhelming responsibility of caring for a tiny human and having no idea how to do that.

My husband was a CEO who constantly travelled and in many ways, I was navigating these early years as a single mum. I'd spent so much of my life thriving in my professional world, where I knew who I was and how to succeed, yet felt completely vulnerable and exposed in this very different world.

What I did know was that from the moment I held Jack,

something inside shifted. I was no longer the center of my own universe, I finally understood what unconditional love meant – not just a concept, I had a living, breathing, life force I was responsible for.

Jack and I were close and I poured my heart into giving him the most wholesome life I could, however, I had to work part-time to help with our finances, so that meant day-care for him.

Over the years he attended more than 15 different centers between the ages of two and four because we travelled so much. Some might shake their heads imagining the instability, however for Jack it was a gift. If you ask him today he'd probably say he learned his social confidence and communication skills in those early years, which helped shape his ability to connect with anyone in any situation.

While I wanted him to adapt to the outside world, I was also intent on nurturing his inner world. I felt his sensitivity early on, and recognized the importance of honoring his emotions.

When driving home from prep school I'd ask him; "How did you feel today? What made you happy, what made you sad?" and he would share his day with me. It was important to me that Jack always felt comfortable expressing his feelings and thoughts.

Sometimes when he didn't feel like talking he'd slip quietly into my counseling room as a silent signal that he wanted to be nurtured through Reiki or Pranic healing with gentle hands, presence and energy to calm his inner turmoil. Those were the moments where communication went beyond language.

As he grew, his sensitivity remained and his intellect blossomed. He was so much like his dad in that regard; sharp, logical and endlessly driven. I also wanted him to have a creative outlet where he could express himself rather than overthinking all the time.

It is important for us all to balance our left and right brain. It is another form of communication to honor our wholeness, not just fixate on one part. It's also not about having to be skilled in the arts or creative activities it's the freedom to express ourselves.

This balancing was difficult for Jack because as a high achiever he was often bullied. Perhaps some of that stemmed from how much attention I gave him and his expectations that others would do the same, and when that didn't happen, it hurt him and he would defend himself with harsh words.

As a mother when we feel our child is hurting and there's nothing we can do, other than to love them through it and help them find their own comfort, it is often a difficult role to play.

High achievers often activate competitiveness or vice versa. Jack's father had been a VFL footballer and the competitiveness of winning was in his DNA. While he modeled this overtly, I carried my own version covertly and Jack was in the middle. Outwardly he was striving to be the best, inwardly he could be fragile when that effort wasn't met with approval or a win!

This is something we all do at times when we are challenged, fail or are negatively judged. Our protection wall comes up and our coping behaviors come out. If only in that moment of the perceived attack, we could breathe and feel our discomfort, before automatically reacting, a far more wholesome response would ensue.

Looking back now, I see parenting Jack was more about learning to communicate in ways that had little to do with language. It was being able to travel through my own upsets and fixed beliefs so I could hear and communicate with him from a clear filter to understand, rather than trying to mold another to understand my values.

On reflection, I probably did the same thing with my husband! All I can say is, when you know better, you do better! As parents I believe it is our authentic demonstration of who we truly are that gives our children the greatest chance to find themselves.

We need to make the space between our words and wounds for the unspoken language of love to surface and, be forever present, as our parenting compass.

 ### *Patterns*

* Over-functioning as a mother to compensate for father's absence and feeling that love equals separation.

* Silent judgment on husband for not being emotionally present, therefore deepening disconnection for both.

* Carrying identity of 'perfect parent' and unconsciously portraying that value comes from how much care is given to others.

* Creating separation by modeling the message that love and acceptance is feminine, and achievement and earning is masculine.

* Not openly expressing frustration to my husband and internally carrying hurts, taught our son to do the same.

* No vulnerability, always coping, acting okay but with no emotional communication – so nobody knew what was really going on inside.

 *Effects*

* Relationships didn't emotionally grow and unspoken burdens became heavier.

* Unbalanced – emotionally, mentally, physically and spiritually – no wholeness.

* Missing the fullness of simple joy of family love by looking after others and not self.

* Missed out on the opportunity to gain a deeper understanding of my child from his perspective, independently of my own.

 *Professional Experience*

Feeling Communication

We experience so many losses due to poor communication over our lifetime, from not being heard during childhood, to being frightened to share real feelings, or perhaps having a louder sibling who drew the limelight. All such things conditioned us to develop coping mechanisms around our spoken words.

Pushing down uncomfortable feelings and emotions is the primary way most of us have learned to cope, as we don't like being out of control and possibly facing an attack. It hurts our heart, so up comes our protective shield and out comes our smile, to keep everyone superficially happy.

Often we use a joke or sarcasm to deflect when anyone has touched our sensitivities, as this raw vulnerability makes us feel uncertain about what to do with it, so, we automatically push it down and mask our hurt with a laugh!

The level we have authentic communication, is the depth we have a real relationship. We often 'hoodwink' ourselves into thinking we are good communicators. I did a session with a manager recently who, when pushed, said; "I think I'm a good communicator, but maybe I'm tricking myself, as certain staff behavior is not changing, no matter how many times I've addressed the problem..."

I shared with her we can have intellectual knowing of our behaviors e.g. *"I know I'm impatient at times but that's the way it is!"* When we only have the understanding from our mind, nothing changes as the true energy is held in our body. If we truly felt what our impatience does to another, we would realize it makes them feel unimportant, unheard, diminished, and that their problem doesn't matter.

This is the reason we need our heart and head combined to be a good leader, not just a manager who ticks all the logical and practical boxes. When we have genuine communication matching our feelings and words, greater trust is formed and people listen.

So many relationships fracture by taking thoughtless words at face value, rather than digging down to a deeper layer of their original emotional source.

I've witnessed couples breaking apart on a single statement – *"I don't love you anymore!"* These five words land like arrows in the heart and instantly, a protective wall is built. In that moment the nervous system leaps into fight or flight and angry, untrue words flow in wounded defense. *"Well I don't love you either!"* or *"I hate you, get out!"* or *"Ok, if that's the way you feel, goodbye!"*

If we were able to pause and breathe, *before reacting*, a completely different outcome would be possible. ***"Alright, tell me what's happening for you to feel like that?"***

When we create safety through openness, the energy changes and remarkable honesty is possible. ***"I feel out of my depth with you, I feel I'm not good enough and would prefer to end it now so I don't get hurt."***

Now we have clearer understanding and no longer have to fight shadows, we are able to move forward with more realness, honesty, and connection to discuss what is possible for the relationship. Whether it stays together or not, both people can move forward with greater compassion and emotional growth.

There are no judgments on any type of relationship as we all have unconscious agreements: we want to get what we want and to give what we want to give. It's part of our physical conditioning as human beings, however, when any relationship depends upon someone staying within your invisible boundaries, where is the unconditional field of love?

 *Client Story*

What Lies Below the Surface?

I recently facilitated a Wellbeing One-Day Workshop with a group of staff from a major retailer. The focus of the workshop was: "The Power of Communication". Here is a glimpse of what transpired...

While all the foundational principles were shared with the group, I could constantly feel this underlying energy, as I facilitated the individuals through different concepts.

As I focused on bridging participants from their current level of awareness into more expanded viewpoints through concepts, roleplays and group exercises, I continued to feel something hovering energetically in the group.

When I started to communicate about being superficial and closed off around our language and only sharing what suits us and feels comfortable, I started to detect an uncomfortable shift in the group energy. I was touching the underlying feeling present within the group, and I needed to open it up.

I started to talk about sitting 'on top of our communications' and only being willing to come through our mind to share, without giving any depth of connection or understanding to people or situations.

I explained how we think this keeps us safe, and that we have this mode of communication on automatic pilot because we think it protects us from getting hurt or being misunderstood.

The room got a little heavier as I provoked the controlling energy in the group, so I got everyone into smaller groups to communicate with each other how they really felt about this concept.

I joined a group with a participant who I thought was operating very superficially. She proceeded to tell me she was open and shared freely and that she was very real in every way.

*I was very direct and said to her; **"That feels like nonsense as I can't relate to anything you just said! You're just saying what you think I want to hear and you are used to people accepting that!"** She burst out laughing, as did the other participant, almost as if I had burst her bubble of untruth and she was actually relieved!*

The whole group felt the prevailing dynamic shift, and everyone started laughing as they all felt freer with the release of the controlling energy, even though they had no idea what had happened.

     ENERGY MATTERS!

This is the unseen, yet highly effective power of group energy. When one truth is broken through, others feel it, and it gives potential for everyone to expand.

I clarified with her she may be sitting on a lot of unspoken emotions and feelings that had been pushed down. She had created a pattern of behavior where she only worked through her mind to supposedly keep her safe, and her heart protected.

The truth is, we only half live when we shut down the most important part of ourselves, our natural, heartfelt connection with self and others.

I could feel her vulnerability, and immediately related it to how fragile we all feel at times, particularly when we experience uncomfortable situations and an inability to cope. We then try and hide behind being tough, controlling or superficial behavior.

As we opened that vulnerable truth between us, we met each other in the space of realness.

It felt like "I know that you know, and you know that I know," and nothing further needed to be spoken. It was never about whether something had been right or wrong, or if we had done something bad or good; all judgments dissolved into the oneness of the moment, when two human beings simply shared their inner truths.

 *Gateway Six*

Communication Exercises

1. Being Present With Communication

Purpose: *To bridge communication to produce better results.*

* What's your intention for the communication e.g. *to tell someone, or to share, or to connect?*

* If you have an agenda and are attached to an outcome, it is difficult to be open and hear the others' perspective.

* See if you can have an expanded intention, of wanting to understand around your communication, rather than being very specific and focusing only on your perspective. e.g. ***"I have ideas on how we should move forward and wondered what you thought, and if there was anything you wanted to add?"***

* Be clear where you are at and what you want from the other person. Remember it is your energy that is picked up first, before you open your mouth. Standing outside the office door, breathe, and ask yourself, ***"What is my intention for this meeting? I want to clearly state where I stand on this project with an openness and check if anyone has any better solutions they could contribute? Once discussed and agreed, we move forward together with our plan in place!"***

Tip: Always put **joint purpose** into place to open the discussion, e.g. ***"I know we both want this to work so we need to understand where each other is coming from."*** And then **LISTEN! This approach will work in your personal life as well.**

Outcome: When we reset into present time, we shift from reacting through old filters into responding with clarity and new possibilities.

2. Active Listening

Purpose: *Deepens empathy, dissolves assumptions and invites a more honest exchange.*

* Say nothing for the first minute in your next conversation.

* Focus on receiving, not mentally preparing your response when the other is talking.

* Listen for their feeling, emotion, where they are coming from beyond their words.

* Is there anything not being said, yet implied?

* Then reflect back, e.g. "Am I understanding correctly that you want to change jobs? Or are you not happy about a particular thing that we could discuss further?"

 The famous philosopher Epictetus said: *'We have two ears and one mouth so that we can listen twice as much as we speak.'*

3. Vulnerability Bridge

Purpose: *Vulnerability gives permission for others to drop their walls creating a mutual field of authenticity and transparency.*

* If we want others to be real, we need to lead by example to establish relationships with greater trust and connection.

✷ It starts with curiosity and willingness to want
to be authentic. It's the ability to be able to share
when we feel uncomfortable, rather than bolstering
our own ego and speaking superficially. E.g. ***"I feel
uncomfortable about addressing this situation, however,
I want the best for you and the team and we need to
establish greater clarity so we can get on the same page."***
Pause and ask how they feel about what you have said
so they feel safe to have honest communication.

4. Communication Mirror

Purpose: *Outcome: Judgments block the energy of the real
message being delivered, but without the block, a clearer
alignment and effective communication will bring about
better results.*

✷ Often what we judge about another person is what
we may be doing ourselves. e.g. You think the other
person doesn't listen to you, however, do you really
listen to them?

✷ When we are judging another, our energy can
be defensive before we start to talk, and this can
increase during the communication. Normally
when this happens the result is not good, as the
other person soon has their protective wall up and
no real understanding penetrates when they feel
under attack.

✷ Tune in to how you would like to be communicated
with, what matters to you and, what makes you
responsive to another's direction and viewpoint.

✷ Write down five actions you believe would make you
a better communicator.

5. Intellect & Heart Coherence

Purpose: *All relationships start to change when we become more authentic and approachable.*

* When our ego is full of intellect and the desire to be right, it is very difficult to be an effective communicator. We may be able to inspire or achieve, however, this only lasts while success is happening and it's dependent on the leader, rather than everyone stepping up and taking responsibility.

* The most effective communication is when the thoughts and feelings combine, so it's not just words heard, they are also felt, and trust is built.

* Open curiosity is required to operate this way. No matter how much we think our ego knows, better results come from being flexible with a caring attitude of wanting to hear what others think and feel.

* We do not have to make others wrong. Rather than stating, *"I don't care what you think, just do it!"* or *"You can get as mad as you like, it's of no consequence, just do your job!"* We can ask, *"What makes you feel that way?"* or *"What part of my communication makes you mad?"* or *"How could we work together to sort out this issue?"*

Extra Exercise

Silent Exchange

Purpose: *To bypass the mind to discover where the deepest communication comes from without words. This is a beautiful exercise to do with a partner.*

* Find a quiet space and sit down facing each other. This is a 2-5 mins exercise of silence.

* Look into your partner's eyes and be still. Even if you laugh at first or feel distracted, come back to present time and continue to look into their eyes without words.

* Focus on feeling them, without judgment. Notice your breath, heartbeat and subtle sensations and simply be with everything as you continue looking into their eyes.

* Afterwards share your experiences with each other from your heart to heart connection.

Write in your journal how you feel after completing these exercises.

The space between the words!

"When we are no longer able
to change a situation, we are
challenged to change ourselves."

Viktor Frankl

Challenges

Pathways Through Barriers

 *Big Picture*

Everyone wants to have a long and happy life, carrying an expectation that things should work out and joy should come easily, whilst pain should be temporary. Yet this very expectation is often the belief that holds us back from deeper soul growth.

Most of us have not been taught about energy and that it is always in flux, shifting between expansion and contraction, highs and lows, joy and sorrow. If happiness existed without contrast, it would no longer be happiness it would simply be a flat, unchanging state.

Without shadow the light has no meaning, and without challenge, there is no evolution.

Let's think back for a moment and recall when we have grown the most?

Was it when we felt comfortable and everything was on track, or was it when life cracked us open, stretched our heart and pushed us to depths we didn't want to go, yet we went, and found another level of ourselves?

Loss is one of our biggest challenges, however, it teaches us so much. Whether it is the death of a loved one, the end of a relationship or the collapse of financial security, loss has a way of stripping us bare!

At first unbelievable, we cling to what we had, then our mind endlessly circles in the 'what ifs' and 'what could have been' to eventually settle in numbness until we are ready to feel again. Sometimes we can stay trapped in this void of loss for lifetimes, or we can choose another path.

Constant blame on someone or something outside ourselves keeps us rooted to our loss, so we need to turn inward and ask; ***"What part of me feels empty over losing***

                    ENERGY MATTERS!

this person or situation?" and when identified, we have a sense of what needs to be healed.

This quiet reflection is available in every challenge and offers a return to our more wholesome self. Beneath our identities, roles and possessions lies a truer version – some may call spirit, soul or sovereignty. Here, we are not separate from our human experiences, yet we understand they are the vehicle we drive to find our way home.

When life throws up challenges it's not really about the challenge, so much as it is the source of our response. Most of us will immediately react and become defensive, overthink, or strategize, to escape the discomfort instead of pausing and tuning in to a bigger picture.

Rarely do we sit with the uncomfortable feeling, be still, think nothing and do nothing, other than simply breathe. What we discover when we are still, is that we become less reactive, calmer, and the fear spike settles, to reveal greater clarity and compassion. Outcomes change coming from this space – whether personally or professionally – as it opens a heartfelt exchange with the person or situation, where greater understanding releases the mind's fixed ideas and expands possibilities.

Our outside world is a mirror to our internal one, and with the social, political, economic and environmental changes we currently face, our inner terrain is constantly changing.

This external uncertainty can crack us open and brings hidden challenges to the surface, to be cleared through awareness and the changing of our old belief systems. This shift aligns us with our natural flow and the greater good.

The outside war is a reflection of the one we wage internally, where we fight ourselves to stay in control through our mind and the 'known' rather than letting our heart resonance (unknown), lead the way and guide us into a whole new workable state of abundance where everybody prospers.

Often we can feel challenge coming before it arrives. This graphic shows when your intuition taps it is wise to listen, rather than bury it. Action what needs to be undertaken, or the original small issue when continually pushed down, rises closer to the surface, and a tiny thing can make us explode.

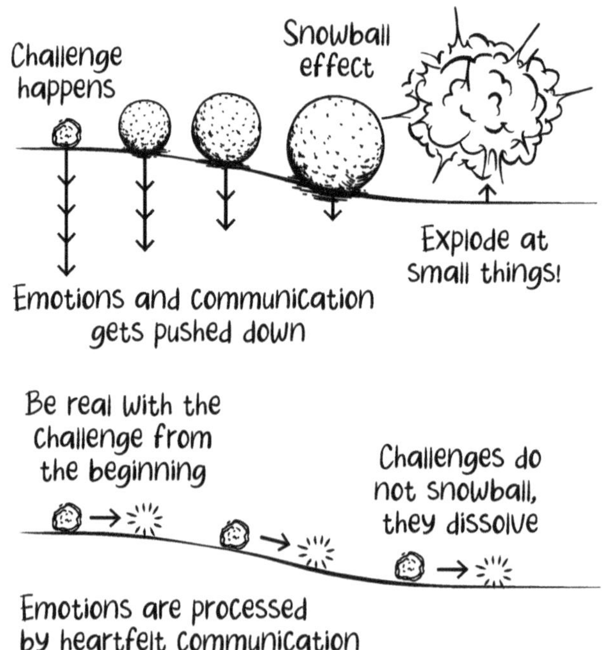

Key Learning: *Life will always challenge us, it is the heartfelt source of our energy that makes the difference to the outcome.*

Personal Experience

On My Own

Being in my fifties and without a home or finances forced me to try and re-invent myself, as the international marketing skills that had served me well in the '80s and '90s became obsolete in the 2000s with the advent of the internet and social media and technology generally taking over! The 'old school' skills I had developed became somewhat irrelevant.

As I was not technically savvy, and didn't understand or relate to computers, it was difficult to get a job, because my resume, like me, was out-of-touch with the fast-moving, technologically-driven social media world I had found myself swept up in.

However, having an entrepreneurial spirit, I nevertheless decided to start my own business. I discovered some exciting health products and with support, created a website. This helped me survive, and I created a traveling retail store, which I took to local markets.

It was a hard life; waking early, packing product into the car, driving long distances and then erecting tents, carrying product, setting up stands, and being alone and on my feet for six hours or more, before packing it all up and driving home. Often there were times when I did well, however there were other dark times when I didn't sell much at all, and as I reflected on my new vocation as I'd drive home late, hungry and tired, I soon came to the realization that I didn't really find it uplifting. I found it a chore!

I have been relentlessly challenged financially and the continued insecurity of not owning a home and being controlled by landlords as a renter has troubled me. The most challenging part is that I was on my own throughout this time, not by choice, just because I'd not found a partner along the way.

Being single and older can be rewarding, as the possibilities are endless and the freedom enjoyable, however, the constant decision-making and not being able to intimately share your life, dreams, or fears, can sometimes make it a lonely place.

All through these times I still believed I could turn things around. I always say, "It only looks like this now, it just hasn't happened YET!" I was going to write a book called *YET* because I feel it is important for us all to keep believing and having hope whilst getting on and being grateful daily for being part of this incredible life experience!

Through all my challenges I have become internally freer as I have had to let go in order to be able to see the bigger picture and to know our external world is created by our internal one.

I don't let my challenges confine me, even when sometimes my head takes over and I fall into overthinking and wondering why my life looks as it does, I don't stay there very long. It's not the real truth; it's just how it physically looks at that moment.

We need to remember that perhaps our time simply has happened YET!

 *Patterns*

* Difficulty adapting to change with a 'new' identity and situation.
* Worrying constantly about financial instability and the future, not present where creation occurs.
* Caught in a linear mindset of having to work hard to create money.
* Stubbornly independent, having to do everything on my own, with strong pride and high expectations.
* No vulnerability to ask for support.
* Overthinking and unworthiness drained trust and self- belief.

 *Effects*

* Being a victim to circumstances made it difficult to create from that energy.
* Constantly being in survival mode without real fulfillment extinguished the joy.
* Underlying loneliness without a partner, emotional support and sharing.
* Always navigating life alone created feeling of being unseen and unsupported – a victim to life.
* Suppressed vulnerability and not sharing true fears and needs with others deepened isolation.
* Overthinking why life looked this way fueled inner anxiety.
* Partial freedom with inner growth, external reality not matching built frustration and spiritual fatigue.

 *'It is not the strongest that survive, but those most responsive to change.'* – Charles Darwin (Naturalist, Evolutionary Scientist)

 **Professional Experience**

Challenge is Breakthrough Point

Every person I've ever worked with comes carrying challenges. It might be an impossible relationship, communication difficulties, a painful life transition, or simply a quiet yearning to break free from old restrictive behaviors. Whatever form it takes, tackling the challenge is always the catalyst to freedom.

Often the current struggle has its roots in childhood and our exposure to untrue beliefs from parents, siblings, teachers, cultural norms, or early environmental influences. They link to misunderstood experiences that have woven restrictive stories into the fabric of our mind.

The challenge is that most of us continue to create and subsequently rely upon these old stories as if they were the absolute truth. We look at life only through our physical lens and continue to justify it as *truth*, evidenced by our experiences. Our conditioning rewards what is visible and measurable, and we hand our power over to the physical, tangible reality, forgetting it is only one layer of a multi-dimensional cosmic system.

When we reduce life to what can be proven, we trap ourselves in the mind's duality of right vs wrong, good vs bad, success vs failure, and with that constant flipping between the two, we wear ourselves out.

The breakthrough comes when we widen the lens and embrace our emotional, mental and spiritual dimensions so we see challenge as a guide, not a punishment. It activates our internal moral compass nudging us back on course, offering expanded awareness of a possible change in direction that needed to happen.

Challenge is not a storm to rail against, instead, it's an opportunity to find another way and to continue to flow with the current by adjusting our sails, rather than getting caught on the riverbank overthinking, and becoming stubbornly stuck.

The true turning point is finding our way back to the core of our heart resonance, the unconditional field of love. From this energy, challenges reveal themselves for what they really are; gentle taps to remind us we are holding on too tightly to someone or something and it's time to let go.

When we embrace this awareness, challenge is never the end of the road. Without fail, it's the beginning of a whole new pathway.

 *Client Story*

Intellectual Awareness Changes Nothing

I am working with a man who has been a business leader for many years. I've known him for a long time and he has achieved a lot in his professional career, albeit peppered with many difficult situations. He contacted me as his life was in turmoil and he felt extremely challenged. Here is his story...

When we started to work together I could feel the fight around letting me access his feelings. When I pressed certain buttons, I was diverted by intellectual knowingness. This is when someone describes the intellectual reasoning of their behavior but goes nowhere near allowing any feelings to emerge.

It's like a smokescreen of words that collectively serve to cause a diversion. It makes you think they are aware of what they are doing, but there is no heartfelt vulnerability or acceptance of how they are really feeling, in order for them to be able to release the contained emotion.

My mentoring sessions are conducted through authentic communication, and I knew he was in there, so I kept penetrating the intellectual ego to try and reach the beautiful human being within and give him a chance to be touched, so he could feel something and start to come out, and open his self-awareness.

He was caught in his own mind and totally associated himself with the harsh group mindset of "winning". Gaining power, money and control over anyone or anything – where vulnerability is seen as weakness and the enemy.

This is a common energy that can attach to us, especially if we have worked in the business world for a long time and we can develop justification for ruthless behaviors to support our belief that everyone is doing the same thing and it's the only way to achieve. At a soul level we are devastated and have no idea why.

These behaviors cover over our true self and make us hard, self-absorbed and separate from our heart. This then extends to our co-workers, partners, families and friends.

All our relationships are unknowingly conducted from this harsh, separate physical/mental energy, and the emotional and spiritual side gets discarded.

We are now in a time where our own untruths are surfacing to be exposed. Anyone who is caught in this type of energy – and we may all be, to a greater or lesser extent – is getting rocked around at the moment.

This old patriarchal mindset is fighting for its life as the truth dismantles this hierarchical reality by the ever-increasing expanded consciousness that is now prevailing.

Even though the client felt a little physically unstable at the end of the session, we were able to unlock the door for his emotional stability to reveal itself.

This will enable him to start to look at how separated he has become from his heart. By not letting himself be vulnerable, he wasn't able to feel the devastating division he had created with those he loved the most! He has now changed that.

 ***Gateway Seven***

Challenges Exercises

1. Being Real With The Challenge

Purpose: *Move from blame to self-responsibility*

1. Write down the challenge facing you, e.g.
    "I'm always living in scarcity."

2. Now write the uncomfortable feelings or judgments
    stirred, e.g. ***"I feel like a failure." "I feel unworthy as I
    can't create worth."***

3. Write against each feeling or judgment the pattern
    that may have created this feeling, e.g. *Failure*

– pattern of expecting to fail, Unworthy – pattern automatically triggered when I don't have enough money means I'm feeling unworthy.

4. Ask what truth lies beyond these feelings and beliefs I've trapped myself in? e.g. *Failure – easier to fail than succeed!* – Not true when I come from my true self. *Unworthy – no pressure from others if I feel unworthy.* – Not true as I have worth as a human being, my mind makes me feel unworthy then I blame others.

2. The "YET"

Purpose: *Reframes Our Energy*

1. Sit quietly and start to notice your breath as you rhythmically breathe in and out.

2. Tune in to your challenge and write or speak out loud what it is, e.g. ***"I'm lonely, I want a relationship, it's been 10 years, what's wrong with me?"***

3. Now add to the end of that statement, **YET!**

4. What would need to change for you to step closer to that happening? E.g. ***"I'm going to learn how to sail, play golf, get good at pub trivia, try something new to break my old patterns of the way I'm looking for a partner."***

5. Where am I coming from inside myself to handle this challenge? E.g. ***"Need someone to make me feel good, so I'm coming from 'needy', not feeling confident and free to have relationship or not!"***

6. What would you need to do to release your needs?

   ENERGY MATTERS!

E.g. ***"Fulfill myself, enjoy and be grateful for life and keep the hope factor open, it just hasn't happened YET!"***

3. A Different Kind of Gratitude

Purpose: *Changing Perspective*

1. Tune in to your heart as this is not about making a list of things you are grateful for to bypass the pain or hurt of your challenge. It's about feeling what and where your body is holding on to your challenge. E.g. ***"I can feel it in my heart."***

2. As you feel the area holding your challenge, talk to it and ask, ***"What is this upset really about?"*** e.g. ***"I feel unloved!"***

3. Say **thank you**: now let's put that aside for a moment and tell the area or organ what you are grateful for about them? E.g. ***"You keep me alive, you pump blood around my body, you give me energy, you give me feelings and emotions and above all, love!"***

4. With this expanded awareness, just let your challenge sit with your body and the intention to help you move through it.

4. Analyze the Challenge

Purpose: *Digging For Gold – Our Greatest Gift Comes From Challenge*

1. Write down your primary challenge, e.g. ***"Can't get a job!"*** Now draw a vertical column down the middle and on one side right all the negative things about challenge. E.g. ***"I feel like a loser, life's not fair, how am I going to get money?"***

2. Now write on the positive side all the awareness
    your challenge has provided for you to learn and
    grow? E.g. ***"I realized I'm going for the wrong jobs, I
    have to change my attitude, I have to listen more and
    talk less, I've got to take more responsibility to be on
    time."***

3. Create five actions you can implement today and
    continue for one month to bring you out of your
    current challenge and closer to your goal.

5. Write a Letter to Your Future Self

Purpose: *Moving Forward*

1. Sit down and let yourself feel and be surrounded
    by your challenge. E.g. ***"I want to write a book and I
    don't feel I can."***

2. Now take a pen and paper and write a letter to
    your future self, 12 months forward in time. E.g.
    ***Dear...., I know you felt overwhelmed and unable to
    write when you first started, yet you put those fingers
    on the keys and typed your thoughts, not worrying
    whether they made sense or not. You got through your
    mind's doubts by taking one step at a time and I'm
    proud of you. You've got this, now keep going!"***

Feel the energy in your letter as if it has already happened and let your life align now into this new creation and your actions will flow!

"Great art is not created through force, but through allowing."

Rick Rubin, legendary music producer

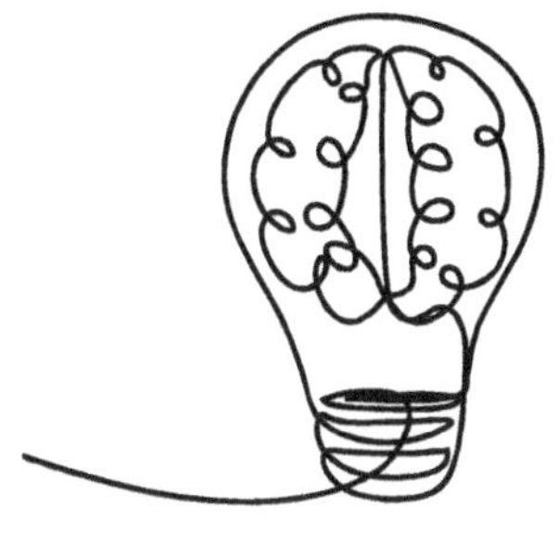

Creativity

The Flow of Conscious Expression

 ***Big Picture***

Creativity is life expressing itself through us. It's not something we do, it's something we tap into and bring through to fruition. It's beyond the mind's control, where energy starts to move with an impulse, spark or sensation and finds its way to form, whether through words, color, sound, touch, taste or action.

It's the language of the soul, far deeper than intellect and flows from the same field that grows a forest, forms a heartbeat and turns a seed into a child. Creativity belongs to all, not just artists; it's a way of problem solving, telling stories, nurturing others, and birthing dreams.

When we create we open the door to the unknown where something new comes into existence and in that moment, we remember we are not separate from the endless stream of life itself. Creativity is not only about art or invention; it's about vision, curiosity, and the courage to bring forth something new.

It depends on our definition and perhaps a bigger picture description is influential – creators not only invented or imagined something new, but they also changed the way humanity saw itself. Think Buddha, Jesus, Lao Tzu, Socrates, Leonardo da Vinci, Albert Einstein, Nikola Tesla, Thomas Edison, Shakespeare, Michelangelo, Beethoven, Rumi, Gandhi, Amelia Earhart, Wangari Maathai, Marie Curie, Martin Luther King Jr, Nelson Mandela, Maya Angelou and Mother Teresa to name a few.

The truth is, everyone is creative in some way, and it's not about fitting into a box, comparing results or fearing judgments, it's about expression! Some of the aforementioned creators continuously let their creativity flow through numbers, equations, testing, and the infinite posturing of ideas, until they finally, cracked the code.

It is the core of our deepest nature as human beings to create, to express, to bring the unseen into being. An idea may spark, however the true magic begins when our energy moves outwards and starts shaping into something to be shared.

When this expression is given to others they can feel the original source, whether through craft, words, sound, food, or performance, as it hits directly into the heart and awakens memory of the creativity residing in all of us.

We marvel at the creation of life itself, how a single sperm fertilizes a single egg and forms the first cell of a human being, developing into a newborn baby, the purest form of the unknown becoming known. Yet as a collective we've drifted away from this sacred creative knowing and prioritized the mind, the intellect, rules and measurable achievements, believing this is a better way to gain security, wealth and power. By doing this, we have undervalued creativity for the priceless natural gift it truly is.

Tune in to the last time you shed a tear. It was probably when you felt someone or something that touched your heart: a movie, a song, words, nature, whatever it was, you experienced your heart resonance reflecting back through a mirrored creation.

Even now as I write these words they arrive from nowhere known. It's a stream of thought flowing through to my fingertips, expressing itself into creation on the page. It comes through with purpose and expands my field of possibilities where more knowingness occurs and new information forms words.

Creativity delivers the greatest gift possible by reminding us we are all connected, all creators, and all part of the same infinite source field, where every act of expression is a thread that weaves us back into the universal tapestry of life.

 *'Imagination is more important than knowledge. Knowledge is limited. Imagination encircles the world.'* – Albert Einstein

 ***Personal Experience***

Pig in Mud

I've always loved creativity. While I've enjoyed crafts, music, design, and writing, it's always been thinking about brand new ideas that I enjoyed the most. Throughout my life, people have constantly asked me to come up with business and personal ideas for them, as I love creating something from nothing!

I think that's where my interest in marketing originated; it was where creativity was about connection, creation, contribution and communion.

However, when it became corporate work, it grew into something else, as the sole intention for creativity became commercialized for the purpose of making money and there was a duality I had to grapple with.

This probably led to my creativity running ahead of me. I would start with a small, simple idea and within a few days, I'd already taken it global in my mind. I used to think that was a strength, and in many ways it was, as I could naturally see a bigger picture, however, I needed to learn that big ideas alone are not enough.

I needed to take responsibility to bring them to life, step by step, and that's where I found it challenging. Maybe it's a metaphor for mind, body, and spirit? The inspiration came from spirit, but I needed my mind and body to ground the ideas and make them real. Whilst creativity begins with individual energy and can be kept to self, it carries further potency when shared with others, as our inner and outer worlds harmoniously connect and uplift everyone with whom our creativity is shared.

In my earlier profession as an international sports marketer, I enjoyed understanding what people wanted and how to package their dreams. After years in corporate work, a deeper love surfaced, one where I wanted to further understand peoples' thoughts and behaviors. This led me to studying psychotherapy and eventually opening a Holistic Counseling Practice in Sydney.

From that point on, my reality started to change along with my priorities and life focus. Even though I earned substantially less, as it takes some time to build up clientele, I felt more valuable and valued.

I gained so much joy from witnessing people's lives change, family love restored, and individuals coming home to their true selves, I didn't care whether I was paid or not; I'd found my passion and purpose.

Every person I worked with exchanged creatively through communication, and I had no idea where we would end up, as present time guided us forward. Together we created a unique pathway to the truth. Creation is an infinite resource available to us all. It's the key that unlocks our imagination, intuition and inspiration, unknown until it is known, and shared!

Letting go of our mind is the key to opening our creativity, enabling the free flow of endless, limitless ideas and insights to form.

 *Patterns*

* Jumping too far ahead by over-idealizing and not staying grounded in practical steps.

* Enjoying the vision, however struggling with discipline, consistency and implementation.

* Allowing outside financial pressures to distort inner values at times.

* Neglecting self-worth through imbalanced mindset of having to be financial before looking after self.

* Difficulty finding middle ground between expansive vision and steady practical progress and systems.

* Sacrificing self and passion by over-emphasis on purpose.

 *Effects*

3. Good ideas lost momentum before materializing, leading to frustration and missed opportunities.

4. Reputation for creativity, however, gap between disciplined budget completion led to failure.

5. Deeper calling compromised by financial needs and commercial viability, which created emotional instability.

6. Undervalued work and accepted less than deserved, lead to exhaustion and lack of self-worth.

7. Doing everything on own with limited resources and technical knowledge, so burnout was inevitable.

 *Professional Experience*

Creativity is often limited in definition to artistry, when in truth it's much broader and far more essential to our wellbeing. I've found that creativity is deeply connected to our flexibility and adaptability of how willing we are to think differently, shift perspectives, and discover new ways of approaching life and work.

I've worked with CEOs, accountants, project managers, doctors and IT professionals to name a few, people often seen as highly intellectual, structured, and 'left-brain wired'. Many would tell me, almost defensively, *"I'm not creative!"*, however, when I observed how they navigated through challenges, I could clearly see creativity in action.

One businessman was convinced he had no creative ability whatsoever, yet the moment he started to problem-solve, you could feel his creative flow intuiting solutions no one else had yet discovered.

In my sessions I love following where peoples' minds want to go. It's fascinating and often deeply revealing, as we uncover the negative beliefs and hidden patterns restricting their growth. When those buried patterns are touched or triggered, resistance often arises to protect against discomfort or vulnerability.

This is human conditioning, however, it's also the very place where creative energy can be blocked and understanding around these points can release the emotion and open the natural creative flow.

We all carry stories, emotions, and experiences embedded in our psyche, and the more we hold onto outdated, untrue storylines, the heavier our burdens become, keeping us trapped in the mind's distorted guidance.

When creative energy is held too tightly, it can be claimed by the ego, whereupon it loses its natural purity and effectiveness. Creativity just like love; it needs to be free to flow in constant giving and receiving cycles of renewal and not held onto tightly like a trophy.

When we hear a singer perform their song live, they must recreate it in that moment, as if it was the first time. It needs to carry heartfelt feeling for their frequency to touch our hearts, and the oneness of their creation to bring us together.

 ***Personal Story***

Love Creation – A personal story for you!

My first instinct is deep emotion as I touch within my heart and become aware of the beauty and the devastation simultaneously.

My physical experience here has been difficult and delightful at times.

It's a very different language spoken here – everything has form, context and confinement, yet the true beauty of nature pervades in every moment.

Stillness is hard to find in the busyness of peoples stories and I get lost and am forgotten.

To survive, I become transactional and form relationships that carry restrictions, and stop me being myself, so I can feel secure and accepted by others.

I separate from my heart, and become physical in order to fit in with how others are living, based on attaching to things to feel safe and in control.

I forget so much that I settle for this game, learn to play it well and think I am enjoying myself and getting what I want. I get to have physical experiences that bring pleasure and it makes me happy.

I like forgetting how my heart feels because I can control things. I have the power to be successful, to be acknowledged, to be important and to be loved, and it suits me, until I feel the loneliness of the emptiness within.

What is that hole, that black void, that fear...? I hate it when it comes up, it makes me feel uncomfortable and vulnerable.

It touches a disliked familiar feeling – "I'm not enough..." "Go away, I am enough – look at my life!" – yet the black hole doesn't listen to my assertions, it unwaveringly persists!

No matter how much I try to get rid of this 'thing' inside of me it remains like a 'thief in the night' wanting to take something from me. I'm not going to surrender to it, I'm going to fight to the death, it's not going to get me!

I continue to enjoy my life, at the same time knowing I also carry this empty 'thing' within that never goes away, it's almost like it's attached to the core of my soul.

I keep my mind in charge to override the feeling, even though it is getting stronger now. I make myself believe I'm doing well, happy, and have what I want. I tell myself I've achieved, I'm important and others who are similar validate this.

However, that stubborn black hole won't release and it's now annoying me, as I can't convince it how good I am. It remains very still, deep, all-pervading and ever-present, elusive in its nothingness.

I hate it, I want to capture it, throw it away, be free of it!

Just let me feel it for a moment, okay... what is happening to me, I cautiously start to feel the black hole and I'm encouraged by something to let go. I start to expand... my mind says stop, but I ignore it and keep opening up. I feel this incredible sense of light, bright, joy, an expanded universe, outside and inside my body.

All of a sudden I break through, like waking up from a deep sleep, I start to know this previously unknown feeling. I ride this sense, as it carries me into a space automatically opening and revealing my source, a familiar feeling of truth, hidden beyond the veils of space, time and story... it's the source of me, my creation, that which holds my physical story...what is this source...? Then I remember, it's LOVE. I AM LOVE!

(PS: While writing this story about love, I looked out my window and a Woolworths truck parked in front of my house carrying a sign on the side saying 'Delivering 7 Days A Week'. I laughed and took a picture of the truck as a metaphor for 'Love being delivered 7 days a week!' Just as it should.)

Next thing I hear a knock on my door, it's the driver asking me if there was something wrong for me to be taking a picture of his truck. I looked at him and told him the truth. I was writing about Love and your truck came along with a poignant message...

He said, "Thank you so much, I've had an awful day and I've been upset, I believe in love and I try my best to give this, however there are a lot of angry people around at the moment."

In that instance we both understood this was no random meeting, it was simply an exchange of love and for us to know we were both on track (or on truck!). We went our separate ways, yet we were united in the same field. The time was 11.11 am.

"We are like islands in the sea, separate on the surface but connected in the deep."– Rumi

 *Gateway Eight*

Creativity Exercises

1. Finding Your Creativity

Purpose: *Tapping into Creativity*

1. Sit quietly, close your eyes and breathe. Imagine a stream of light moving through the top of your head through your body, like a ray of sunshine.

2. Without thinking, start writing or expressing the feeling of this light and note whatever impulses arise.

3. Now read or reflect on what emerged without judgment and simply acknowledge the energy that wanted to come through you.

2. Spontaneous Creation

Purpose: *To Create Flow Rather Than Task*

1. Choose an everyday activity e.g. cooking, walking, planning, dressing and decide to do it in a way you've never done before. e.g. *Cooking, if you normally follow a recipe, let yourself cook from instinct and create a new dish.*

2. Notice the sensations that arise when stepping into the unknown, perhaps *doubt, freedom, overwhelm. Write down what you discovered about your flexibility and adaptability along with your hidden strengths.*

3. Clearing Old Blocks

Purpose: *Remove Creative Blocks*

1. Write down three stories or beliefs you've been carrying that limit your creativity, e.g. ***"I'm not creative." "I need to be perfect." "I can't make money from my ideas."***

2. Slowly read each belief aloud and notice when/ where the body tightens.

3. Now read again and breathe deeply on the exhale, saying, ***"I release this old story and bring my energy into the flow of now."***

4. Against each old belief write a new belief and firmly cross out the old one as it is now obsolete.

4. Bringing Creativity to Form

Purpose : *Inspiration to Grounded Action*

1. Think of an idea you would like to explore. Break it into three small steps you could do this week.

2. Do one step at a time and when this action is taken, observe that your creation is now coming in form.

3. When you have completed the three steps, put together your next three steps. Don't just write them down, feel what you are writing, now put them into action.

4. Now imagine your idea being completed. How would it look and feel to be in the flow of your creation and to be sharing it with others?

5. Sharing Your Creation

Purpose: *The Potency of Shared Expression*

1. Create something right now e.g. A poem, words to a song, floral arrangement, drawing, invention, business idea, book to write.

2. Now share your creation/idea with another person. Notice how you feel and what your mind does with this.

3. Write down your experience and how you could keep going to create more of the same in your life.

4. People want to exchange with, and connect to, your energy! You have something to share and it's time to share it!

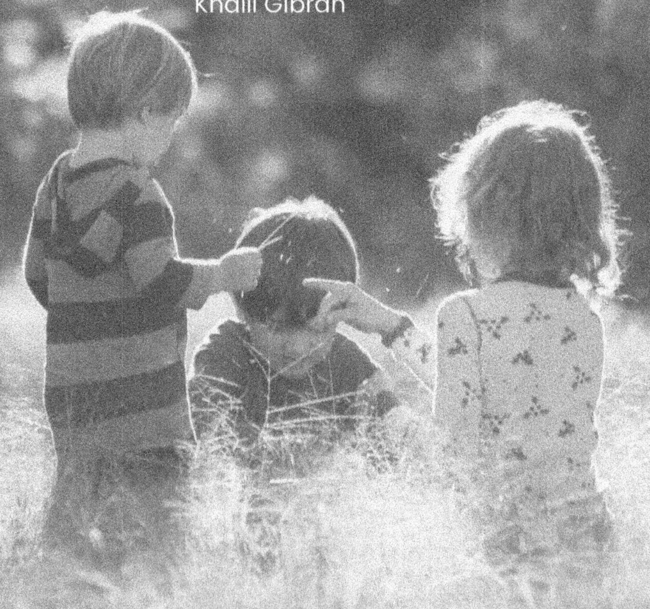
"Your children are not your children.
They are the sons and daughters
of Life's longing for itself."

Khalil Gibran

Restoration of Original Love

Key to Finding the Unconditional Within

Big Picture

What if we didn't just arrive here by chance? What if, on a soul level, we chose our parents, not only to receive their love, but to help heal generational wounds and beliefs they couldn't? In doing so, we entered families with deep-rooted patterns, not to suffer under them, but to eventually awaken and rewrite them.

As a newborn we come into this incarnation carrying subtle imprints, strands from past lifetimes, ancestral patterns, and soul agreements made before birth. From the very first breath, beliefs begin to shape us, both those we arrive with, and others we absorb instantly from the world around us.

As we start to grow these influences affect us particularly if love is withdrawn or not available from parents. We automatically feel unlovable and unknowingly make decisions e.g. *Shut off and protect self* or *I'm going to hide my love to stay safe.*

Have you ever thought what was happening for your mother or your father when you were born? What were they going through emotionally, mentally, physically and spiritually?

We want our parents to be there for us and when they are unable, we unconsciously shut down our love and block them out because they have hurt us and we automatically feel unlovable, which translates to *our love is not enough.* This is where we need to heal our own wounds.

Disconnection from any original family member can padlock our love. The key to open it is often elusive and deeply buried beneath extreme sensitivity and hurt.

Rejection is the bullseye for the painful arrow we've carried for lifetimes, and the shutdown point of our love.

While we can cope with physical separation from our original family, nobody copes well with spiritual separation, as it is not the truth. Even if there has been trauma and terrible behaviors, there is still a being with a heart that we are connected to by our original choice. Whoever is aware is the one who can move first by letting go, and opening their heart metaphysically – even if there is no physical contact, it frees our love.

It's from freedom our true nature flows, needing no protection, nor attack, as it is the source of our sovereignty and joins the missing links between our physical and spiritual connections into the oneness of love, from which we are born and return to.

This is why it is important to restore love in families as it relates to our purpose of being here. It's a personal awareness of the nature of our heart's resonance, which is constantly open. It's our mind's perception that supposedly closes it down. It's our ability to see the human 'being' beyond their negative behavior as we have all been conditioned, some more than others. We can't change anyone else and we can disagree with their behavior, however, when we reside in our true self, it's impossible to close our heart frequency to anyone.

It matters not whether the person is physically present, as this is an energetic shift which restores the generational love-lines carried through time and space.

Personal Experience

Not What It Seems

In my own family I have an older sister and two younger brothers and I sense our love bonds were formed as children. They were healthy, living in a warm, loving family with a wholesome mum and dad. Love flowed freely and we lived a simple life, full of fun, work and celebrations.

In my teens things changed. My sister left at 21 to be married, and I moved to the other side of the country to investigate work opportunities, leaving my two brothers at home.

We all lived separate lives, albeit there were many visits home to see Mum and Dad. As the years rolled by and our mum passed, we began to have less contact, then our dad passed and the physical connection lessened further, with me on one side of the country and them on the other. This upset me, as I always wanted our family to be close and this physical distance made it challenging to demonstrate our loving bond with each other.

What I have come to realize subsequently, is that it is not about the amount of physical contact, it is more about the quality of connection with each other, and it requires effort to keep that alive.

Even though my visits back home are infrequent, the genuine love we have for each other is deeply felt and when we do connect, we speak the same language, in the original family way of recalling fun stories of being together as siblings, the adventures shared, and simple love!

Mums, dads, children and siblings all have behaviors we get caught up in, where our focus changes to what we are personally going through and it can feel like separation, indicating, at least perceptually, that we are not loved. What can then happen is we get hurt and take it personally, so in defense our response is to shut our love down.

Our natural love flow that constantly exists gets denied and each person stays in their own world thinking they are separate, unless one is aware of what is happening and keeps their love open and flowing without pride, ego, hurt, and resentment getting in the way. This is not denying that someone's behavior is unacceptable, it is keeping your heart open to make your decisions and actions.

It's a challenging thing to do, particularly with family, however it's part of us remembering our purpose for being here and the sound of our ancient, familiar tune, ever present deep in our heart so that even when separated we are still all one.

 *Patterns*

* Taking things personally rather than understanding what is happening for/to another person.

* Holding untrue beliefs that I was not loved.

* Thinking something was wrong with me if siblings were not in contact.

* Wanting my mother's love so I would be inauthentic to self.

* Not seeing my parents' emotional difficulties, stuck on self.

* Lived in my own world of importance and ego.

 *Effects*

* Made up my own stressful situations by making assumptions.

* Tried to do more things physically so I would deserve more love.

* Would contact people to push for connection which made me feel more unloved.

* Became controlling with my love and used it to manipulate which distanced people.

* True emotional availability was limited by not feeling what was happening for others.

* Had no bigger picture, stayed in physical life to gain rather than give, causing separation.

 *'Relationships are the agents of change, and the most powerful therapy is human love.'* – Dr. Bruce Perry, Neuroscientist & Child Trauma Specialist

 *Professional Experience*

Child Beingness

Most people I work with carry wounds around family love, as parents, children, or siblings. In session, I often hear:

* *"They don't want me in their life, and I don't want them in mine."*

* *"I've shut them out for my own health."*

* *"They need to pay for what they've done to me."*

* *"I can't deal with them anymore."*

At first, these statements feel final, but when we journey deeper, a different truth begins to surface. Wherever families have separated, there is always a thorn of hurt, a place of incompletion. Often this wound is not only personal but generational, passed down through family lines and unconsciously repeated.

I worked recently with a father estranged from his two sons. He held tightly to the belief that they had hurt him, while they held firmly to their story that he had hurt *them*. Both sides stood in stubbornness, unable to forgive and move through their pain. In these moments, love feels locked behind walls of justification.

By contrast, I also worked with a 25-year-old man whose father had been absent and a poor role model in his life. This young man chose to see beyond his father's failings, recognizing both his father's human flaws and his spiritual essence. He understood that his father had endured his own painful childhood and simply didn't know how to be a parent. This wasn't about excusing his harmful behavior, it was about opening to compassion, awareness, and understanding that none of us are perfect, and nor are we meant to be.

When the son let go of his understandable upset through awareness, something shifted. His father felt a safe, open, non-judgmental space and he could feel his heart, long closed by his own wounds, and he began to soften. What unfolded was not just a reconciliation of two people, but a reunion of love that had always been there beneath the story. The ripple effect of that reunion flowed through the entire family.

This is the nature of generational healing. When one person takes the courageous step to release their protective patterns and untrue beliefs, it creates space for others to do the same. I see it again and again; the moment one member of a family opens, healing becomes possible for all.

The truth is, most of us have been parented by people who themselves carried wounds, cultural, emotional, hereditary, or simply unspoken patterns of fear, and beliefs they are unlovable. These patterns are passed along from parents to children to relationships until someone chooses differently. Restoring family love doesn't have to be complicated, it begins with whoever is ready to move first, not because they have to, because they *want* to.

Often children wait for parents to change, however in reality, the healing can unfold in many ways, like a code unlocking in perfect sequence. What matters most is willingness! Every time one person chooses love over separation, they not only restore connection within their family, but they also reinstate more of their own authentic self by healing their heart as part of the greater good.

In this way, family love is not just about mending broken relationships so much as it is about aligning with the deeper truth of who we are. Through unconditional love, we return to the natural, universal pattern of giving and receiving that connects us as humans, and ultimately, as one humanity.

 Client Story

Love of the Father

This beautiful young man was happy to share his story with you.

Together we cried and laughed through the session as he unraveled the days before his father's passing. He touched my heart so deeply as he shared the emotional rollercoaster of his feelings and upset at what he experienced.

He told me how happy he was that he had restored love with his father and that they had spent the last year of his life reacquainting themselves with each other, saying all the things they wanted to say to each other and realizing how much they had always been in the other's heart, whilst he lived in Australia and his father in the UK.

Originally this young man had come to me about an emotional issue that was affecting him physically, and he was finding it difficult to live a normal life.

Throughout his visits to me he travelled through different mindsets he was caught in, where overthinking had caused overwhelm and doubt, leaving him feeling disconnected from everyone, including himself.

From my notes – 'Jason' feels awkward and not sure how to be around his father. He felt disappointed in his Dad and his behaviors. All these words came up as we travelled through the feelings he held in his body that had been suppressed – confused, love/hate, stuck, lost, trapped, doubt, stubbornness, scared, making excuses and finally, in the letting go of the underlying belief, (probably formed as a child), ***"I'm scared to be vulnerable as I'll get hurt!"***

He released himself, demolishing the 'Jenga Tower' of negative blocks, dismantled his mind's creation and all he was left with was love.

He had parked his love for his father off to the side and got on with his life, accepting they would always be estranged, however, it continued to gnaw away at him, literally. That's when he originally came to me about a different emotional issue that was masking the root cause, which was separation from his father.

He came to see me again soon after his father had passed. This beautiful young man was so happy he had restored the love with his father, who drew his final breath in a hospital bed in the UK, whilst his son was lying in his bed, holding the picture of his father in Sydney.

He told me he suddenly felt a tap on his shoulder, and immediately sensed it was his Dad who had come to be with him (in Australia) to say "goodbye". In that very moment, the phone rang, and a kind, gentle voice let him know "Your Dad has gone!"

He knew where his dad had gone, he had come to be in his heart where they would forever be ONE.

 *Gateway Nine*

Restoration of Original Love Exercises

1. Before You Were Born – Reframing

Purpose: *Shift blame to curiosity and see parents as human beings with their own inner story*

1. Find a quite space for 10 mins, close your eyes and breathe gently.

     ENERGY MATTERS!

2. Firstly picture your mother at the moment you were born. Imagine her face, hands, age, energy, and life situation. Don't edit the image, just allow the sensations to come.

3. Ask softly *"What was happening for you when I was born? What fears, hopes or pain were you carrying?"* Wait for impressions to arise through small feelings, images and words.

4. Hold these visuals and feelings with compassion, not judgment; if there is any resistance, simply observe it.

5. Finish by placing your hand over your heart and saying any words you feel appropriate e.g. *"I see you, I release my need to be hurt by what I thought you were. I open to the possibility of your human struggle and I thank you for having me."* or *"I know you wanted me despite the emotional struggles you were facing. I understand and am grateful to you for birthing me into this world, thank you, Mum."*

6. Now do the same exercise again with your father or other parent. Find your own words in point five from your heart you would like to say. e.g. *"I know you wanted me and I understand you were focused on how you were going to provide for us which made you harsh at times and I release my untrue belief that you didn't love me."*

2. The Shift From "Me" to "Them"

Purpose: *Changing our perspective beyond our personal hurt*

1. Write down what you believe your family member
    has *"done to you."* Be specific, even with an example
    of their behavior that hurt you as this will help you
    to gain greater insight.

2. Ask them this question, *"What might have been
    happening for you at this time emotionally, mentally and
    physically?"*

3. Write down at least three possibilities, even if
    you don't believe them fully as this opens up
    compassion to understand they may have been
    struggling too, not just acting against you.

3. Spot The Pattern – Not the Person

Purpose: *Many wounds come from repeating family patterns*

1. Think of one repeating behavior you notice in
    your family e.g. shutting down, anger, withdrawal,
    jealousy, competitive, emotional avoidance, scarcity
    mindset, egotistical, rebellious.

2. Write down when you have seen this in your parent,
    sibling, child or self.

3. Now see where you have shown the same pattern,
    even in a different form or a different time.

4. What have you become aware of and are prepared
    to do to change this? Write down your thoughts.

4. The Open Door

Purpose: *Sometimes connection feels broken, however love is still there*

1.   Imagine there's a closed door between you and your family member.

2.   Draw a line down a sheet of paper and write on the left side what your hurts, needs and protection might be.

3.   Then write on the right side, what their hurt, needs and protection might be?

4.   What have you become aware of and write down three steps you would be prepared to take, to move you forward.

5. Our Human Being-ness

Purpose: *To understand that our bad behaviors come from our controlling mind, however, our being-ness holds our unconditional love*

1.   We are going to write two short letters that will not be sent, however they are very important to be written. Letter One – Address the person you feel separate from and write down their behavior that upset you, what it felt like and the impact it had on you.

2.   Letter Two – Now tune in to their being-ness, who you truly know them to be and write from your heart, to speak to their heart.

3.   Write down what you have become aware of and if there is any action you feel moved to do, physically or spiritually?

"Who looks outside, dreams;
who looks inside, awakens."

Carl Jung

SUMMARY

The Veil Lifts

Freedom, Truth and Love is Revealed

 ***Big Picture***

We may be living in the most extraordinary and pivotal time this planet has ever known.

Everything is shifting: our sense of time, planetary rhythms, economic, political, social, and environmental structures combined with the rise of AI, is creating a unique speed of change, as the world struggles to reorganize itself in real time.

These changes are disrupting life as we know it. They are also creating a separation between those who are willing to rise with curiosity, open hearts and a willingness to step into a new truth for the greater good, and those who want to hold on to old mind-made ways of the patriarchal system.

We are all standing at the crossroads, we can say 'no' and hold onto our old beliefs, behaviors and burdens we've carried for lifetimes, or, we can say 'yes' and step into a greater reality where our inner and outer worlds reflect one another, where what we do to others we ultimately do to ourselves and where we finally remember that we were never separate.

When we return to our heart's natural power of resonance, something remarkable becomes possible. We may experience time differently, like leaping timelines and finding ourselves returning to what we have always carried deep within, the memory of love and our alignment with this reality.

How Can We Do This?

It begins with something simple, gratitude for life itself, the beauty of this planet, appreciating each day as a new experience, the gift of being alive and that it is freely given.

How we value that gift and what we choose to do with it shapes everything. When we reconnect with this truth the illusion loses power.

Love moves effortlessly, abundance flows, connection returns and we remember that we were never meant to stand alone – we were always part of one shared life!

What if Lily and Gabe walked among us and maybe, just maybe, you met them. Could you help them to remember the source of who they are, by remembering your own tune?

When we move through life guided by the heart, the unknown becomes less daunting and the path ahead becomes more familiar. Just as the whale calls its pod home across the oceans of time and space, we too are being called home.

We are each being invited to take our place and play our harmonic note in the universal orchestra of life and maybe, this is the most important time in history, where our energy really matters!

Thank You!

It's taken a long time sitting in hundreds of cafes around Australia, drinking too many flat whites, as I scribbled and pondered the meaning of life in my tattered notebook.

When I finally put my fingers on a keyboard the words flowed, unknowingly becoming my friend as they helped unravel my life personally and professionally. It has been cathartic for me, as I hope it has been for you.

We all have a story and I hope this encourages you to share a greater awareness of yours, not only the external one, but more importantly, your inner one, often not recognized or expressed.

When one person has the courage to open their awareness and change, it encourages others to do the same, our perceived separation drops away, and we are all connected with a greater truth.

If you enjoyed reading your way through these pages, even if it challenged you, I believe NOW is the time to take your seat and start playing your harmonic note as part of the divinely orchestrated field of unconditional love, because your ENERGY MATTERS!

Big Picture Summary

Gateway One – Remembering

From the moment we are born, we are taught to seek ourselves in the mirror of others.

We quickly learn that if our mum smiles, we must be good, and if our dad withdraws, we've done something wrong. Praise becomes proof of worth, and this mindset makes us desperately seek approval as a way of validating our existence. By constantly looking outwards for our value we quickly become conditioned to operating in the mind's duality of good vs bad and right vs wrong, where our performance becomes a measure of feeling loved or feeling worthless.

Our parents were not told and nor did they tell us that simply 'being' our natural self is enough. It is the beginning point of life. The power of being present with our internal world, by default, creates our external one. Feelings are our Geiger counter, and whether good or bad, we need to feel and release them, so they are not pushed down and stored in the mind and body.

Our parents didn't tell us, because it was never said to them, "You are here because you chose to be here. We are so happy you chose us and we will help you to remember, to heal, to feel your way through your experiences so you can have your own adventures while walking through the illusion and finding your way home."

Instead, we teach our children to look outside themselves and to learn to be reactive to life. To protect through forming barriers, to chase meaning through action, productivity, perfection and to barricade themselves in, often to become someone they are not.

When we experience negative actions against us, we get hurt, feel uncomfortable and can become resentful, thinking there is something wrong with us. To feel okay again, we push the feeling down which creates a little knot inside and we continue to do this every time we feel emotionally uncomfortable. **The first step for us is to undo the knots so we can start to feel comfortable with being ourselves again.**

Gateway Two - Drivers Seat

Those knots get tied when we grow up learning to behave a certain way and are rewarded for it. If we follow the 'right' path, as set out by others, we'll be accepted and without realizing it, we give our power away to external forces. We become conditioned to believe life is something that happens to us, rather than something we create!

Let's look in the rear vision mirror of our life and see when we've been riding along as passengers and blamed the driver for where we ended up!

One of the biggest reasons so many of us feel off track, stuck, frustrated, or powerless, is because we've been conditioned to look outside ourselves for both the cause of, and solutions to, our problems.

Unconsciously we start to become dependent on everything changing outside before we can feel okay. If someone hurts us, we shut off and blame them for the way we feel. Until *they* change, nothing can change.

By adulthood these beliefs run deep and blame is part of life. We blame the economy, partners, parents, bosses, even our children for not delivering what we want. It is much easier to blame than to take self-responsibility for the experiences we have created.

This is how we end up in the passenger seat of life. We hand control over to circumstances, routines, expectations, and other people's opinions. We react to what's happening around us instead of creating what we truly want. At times life can feel like a series of unpleasant detours we didn't choose, roads we didn't map and destinations that take us a long way from home.

On the surface this can appear perfectly normal as most of us are living this way. However many feel a relentless emptiness within that something is missing. Even if on the surface we are happy, we question; "Is that all there is?"

Transformation begins when we shift our focus from pointing outward to inward, and start owning, instead of blaming. This isn't about beating ourselves up! No, it's about recognizing we are responsible for our choices, beliefs, energy, and actions, which shape the life we are living.

With this awareness, we take back the wheel and drive in the direction that feels most authentic and real. However it's not always easy and means questioning long-held stories and beliefs we've created and inherited.

It means coming out of automatic pilot mode and being present with the negative thoughts that have affected self and others. We have unknowingly – or knowingly – hurt people and not taken responsibility for our actions.

If we want the negative energy to release, we need to be willing to feel, understand and care about what that hurt felt like for others, and ourselves, as a consequence of our thoughts and actions.

Some may think; *"Why should I do that? They hurt me first!"* However, it takes one person to open up the truer connection beyond mindset behaviors. As human beings we have all been trapped in the physical duality field of right and wrong which makes us judge others, rather than being curious to explore how we can harmonize our different viewpoints.

This raises our integrity and the only place we're truly in the driver's seat is with our heart resonance – that's our engine room! From this source we are able to see ourselves and others, beyond our everyday behavior, and realize that all human beings really want, is to connect, as that is our true nature.

Our lives have never been out of our hands, we just believed they were and the moment we truly understand and dispel this belief is the moment everything changes. As our inner world starts to align, our outer world begins to shift and ignites the process of dissolving old negative patterns to expose a clearer pathway forward. **We were never meant to be passengers; we were born to drive!**

Gateway Three – Natural Connection

As we drive forward we can become very physical and think of ourselves as flesh and bone, yet beneath the surface of our human form, we are, at our core, energy in motion.

Every cell and atom in our body is made up of particles, electrons, protons and neutrons constantly moving and vibrating. The quantum field isn't some 'out there' concept, it's right here within us, pulsing with every heartbeat. We are living expressions of energy in physical form.

Long before concrete and clocks, we lived in rhythm with Earth and her celestial bodies. We honored them, not as distant objects, but as family. We danced under full moons, planted according to the lunar cycles, rose with the sun and offered gratitude to the stars.

But what if Mother Earth was the jewel in the crown of our solar system and she had fallen out of universal alignment because of our disharmony?

Over time we started to forget to value, listen, nurture and care for her, instead we 'mined' her as if she was a commodity to be taken for granted and her resources endlessly used for our personal gain.

If we stopped and listened for a moment we might hear her whisper, whether through birdsong, a tree rustle, a water splash, or even the warmth of our breath. Pause... We can feel her presence consciously or unconsciously, in every cell. Nature holds the 'forever background' frequency while our human story commands our foreground presence and attention. **When we sense this greater connection and attune our frequency with nature's energy, she becomes responsive to us.**

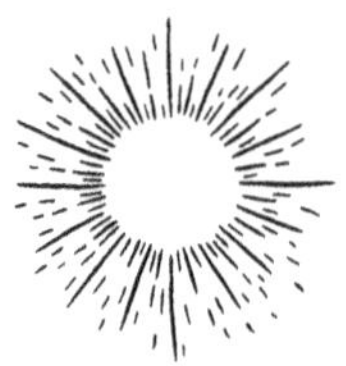

Gateway Four – Untrue Belief Systems

Imagine waking up one day and realizing we had been living inside a giant belief system, almost like a movie set, without knowing. From birth we are handed the script of what to believe, how to behave and what success looks like.

Our world is then created by humanity's collective belief patterns, where thoughts have formed actions, and actions have become words recorded as 'truths'. Yet these inherited 'truths' have subtly limited us from realizing the boundless possibilities that exist beyond them.

Everyone forms their own interpretation, purely based on how much they need to belong to the group, or alternatively, how free and authentic they individually want to be.

We are energy and naturally flow in symbiosis with all living things, so when fixed beliefs are conditioned into our mind, they form barriers to expansion and our ability to adapt to our ever-changing world.

Our mind blocks our capacity to flow, and throws us into a black-and-white reality where logic is used against love and it becomes more important to gain, rather than give. The chance of loss raises our fears, spurring us on to fight harder, to build stronger internal resistance, to cling to things, and for the intellect to block the heart's resonance.

Some may say the Bible, or similar religious tomes, creates a set of beliefs, and corresponding stories, to give us a reference point of what it means to be a human being living on earth at any particular time.

For instance; 'An eye for an eye' found in the Old Testament of the Bible (Exodus 21:24), states that retaliation is justified. However, in the New Testament, Jesus moved from justice to mercy, non-retaliation and transformation over conflict. This higher belief shifts from protecting fairness, to breaking the cycle of harm altogether.

It is only by turning inwards, by meeting the parts of us we've hidden, or dismissed, that we begin to liberate ourselves from inherited restriction. When we shine light on old wounds and dissolve our coping behaviors, we begin to emerge, present, powerful and wholesome.

When we get upset about someone or something, we have unknowingly touched our inner fear as we feel some kind of attack. Someone has a different belief system to ours and because we think our system is the best, our mind fights against others who would rock the boat and disturb our secure world. Rather than addressing our discomfort, we blame and try to change the other person.

This blame encourages us to divide into tribes, territories, countries, and erect boundaries to assert the final separation. To keep these beliefs in place, we make others our enemy, and chose to fight them to gain more power, as greed and money drive us forward.

It also encourages acquisition and ownership, not sharing, and abandoning the notion of common unity for the greater good. We ended up in a linear world, heads full of limitations, asserted restrictive thoughts, and egocentric behaviors with matching actions and results.

Group-mind beliefs have developed into fixed rules humanity is now rebelling against, as they are based on control and restriction, to erode our freedom of spirit.

Gateway Five – Inner Senses

Our freedom of spirit transforms when we awaken to our true sensory capacity, not limited to five, but limitless as all are doorways into deeper understanding of the self.

How often do we pause long enough to notice our breath? If we did, how long could we stay present, clear minded and let our thoughts float by like clouds?

In the same way, when was the last time we truly listened to our body, not just when it aches or fails us, but when it is quietly sustaining our life, moment to moment?

Are we ever aware of our lungs expanding and contracting, our heart pulsing, our cells circulating and our bones holding us upright? Probably not, it just happens for us! Maybe it's time to thank our internal organs for the great job they are doing?

Too often we only notice the body when something goes wrong, when we resist, complain, feel unfairly treated and forget the constant miracle of everything going right in every second of our existence.

In moments of stress or difficulty, the mind quickly takes over and catastrophizes, criticizes, compares and fills us with endless 'what ifs'. One moment our mind undervalues us, telling us we are hopeless or not enough, the next it overvalues us, inflating us with superiority. Yet both are illusions of the same thing, the absence of genuine self-love.

The more we turn inward and sense beyond the noise, we begin to hear a deeper calling. We start to realize our external world mirrors our internal one.

For example, what we see on the surface of a tree the trunk, leaves and branches, yet this is only part of the picture. The real life force flows underground, in the unseen root system, sustained by hidden networks that nourish its visible beauty.

The same is true for the health of our inner landscape as it is determined by the nurturing quality of our thoughts, emotions and energy. The external world is only a reflection to highlight where we are flowing and where we are depleting ourselves. With our focus outside ourselves, we disconnect from our inner guidance and become unnatural, blocked versions of self.

When we pay attention to the clues the body gives us, a tight chest, a heavy stomach, a wave of tingles, we are really listening to the language of the universe flowing through us. I'm sure you can relate when you hear someone singing a beautiful song and it sends goose-bumps through us as the external vibration meets our internal vibration.

This demonstrates the importance of looking after ourselves and being aware of what we put into our bodies, the relationships we engage with and the environments we place ourselves in.

Every choice ripples through our inner landscape and out again into the greater field. Caring for ourselves is not a small, private act, it's the symbiosis of life, and it matters.

Gateway Six - Communication

In this symbiosis communication is more than words. It's an exchange of energy, an invisible current that creates harmony or separation between someone or something. At its best, it manifests common union, a shared space where connection, understanding, and trust naturally grow.

Our very first communication begins not with another, but with ourselves. As babies we cry, not from learned words or social conditioning – it's from raw expression, need, truth, and life force we hold deep within.

This is our original source and as we grow, it colors how critical or compassionate we are with ourselves and others. When our inner dialogue is honest and aligned our sharing carries this resonance and people hear and feel our words.

When the source of words is solely spoken from the mind they can feel cold, hollow or disconnected. They may be technically correct, however, they lack the ability to penetrate the heart and be remembered. When words have warmth and are true, they are received at a deeper level and are likely to be acted upon.

Every relationship whether personal, professional

or intimate is built on communication. With each exchange we either strengthen the bond through building connection, or weaken it through separation. Sometimes we judge someone's words and filter them through our belief system, forming immediate opinions that can block us from receiving *their* message.

Flexibility and curiosity are key. For instance, if you don't understand or agree with what someone has said, you could say; ***"I'm not sure I understand, could you share that another way, as I genuinely want to connect with you?"*** Spoken with sincerity, this approach evokes trust and greater understanding.

This requires moving beyond ego where everything circles back to us. We need to be genuinely interested and attentive to the other person. Real communication begins in a shared field of respect, where two people work together to create a wholesome connection.

The way we communicate determines the quality of our relationships. If we stay superficial, sarcastic, or guarded, our connections will reflect that. If we bring honesty, vulnerability, and genuine care, those same qualities will echo back to us. Communication mirrors the energy and intention we bring to it.

Many people believe they need 'different' communication styles for work and home however this belief often creates a false dichotomy within us. The truth is, we are the same human being wherever we go, no labels required. Whether speaking to a colleague, a partner, or a child, the most powerful words come from the same heartfelt source of trust, respect, and authenticity.

Even in high-stakes conversations, integrity wins. We all have inner radars that can detect when something feels 'off'. Our body talks, the gut tightens, our heart senses a lack of congruence and our intuition speaks to us softly; "It's not true!" These subtle unspoken signals are just as powerful as the spoken word, and when they don't align, we have a communication breakdown.

When we allow our heart intelligence to guide our words, something remarkable happens. Communication shifts from simply being an exchange of words and information to a meaningful sharing of a harmonious tune.

The other person hears and feels us, which creates space for new possibilities. **Conversations become transformative, turning simple exchanges into opportunities for deeper relationships, collaboration, and that's when the magic happens!**

Gateway Seven – Challenges

Everyone wants to have a long, happy, magical life, carrying an expectation that things should work out and joy should come easily, whilst pain should be temporary. Yet this very expectation is often the belief that holds us back from deeper soul growth.

Most of us have not been taught about energy and that it is always in flux, shifting between expansion and contraction, highs and lows, joy and sorrow. If happiness existed without contrast, it would no longer be happiness it would simply be a flat, unchanging state.

  ENERGY MATTERS!

Without shadow the light has no meaning, and without challenge, there is no evolution.

Let's think back for a moment and recall when we have grown the most?

Was it when we felt comfortable and everything was on track, or was it when life cracked us open, stretched our heart and pushed us to depths we didn't want to go, yet we went, and found another level of ourselves?

Loss is one of our biggest challenges, however, it teaches us so much. Whether it is the death of a loved one, the end of a relationship or the collapse of financial security, loss has a way of stripping us bare!

At first unbelievable, we cling to what we had, then our mind endlessly circles in the 'what ifs' and 'what could have been' to eventually settle in numbness until we are ready to feel again. Sometimes we can stay trapped in this void of loss for lifetimes, or we can choose another path.

Constant blame on someone or something outside ourselves keeps us rooted to our loss, so we need to turn inward and ask; ***"What part of me feels empty over losing this person or situation?"*** and when identified, we have a sense of what needs to be healed.

This quiet reflection is available in every challenge and offers a return to our more wholesome self. Beneath our identities, roles and possessions lies a truer version – some may call spirit, soul or sovereignty. Here, we are not separate from our human experiences, yet we understand they are the vehicle we drive to find our way home.

When life throws up challenges it's not really about the challenge, so much as it is the source of our response. Most of us will immediately react and become defensive, overthink, or strategize, to escape the discomfort instead of pausing and tuning in to a bigger picture.

Rarely do we sit with the uncomfortable feeling, be still, think nothing and do nothing, other than simply breathe. What we discover when we are still, is that we become less reactive, calmer, and the fear spike settles, to reveal greater clarity and compassion. Outcomes change coming from this space, whether personally or professionally, as it opens a heartfelt exchange with the person or situation, where greater understanding releases the mind's fixed ideas and expands possibilities.

Our outside world is a mirror to our internal one, and with the social, political, economical and environmental changes we currently face, our inner terrain is constantly changing.

This external uncertainty can crack us open and brings hidden challenges to the surface, to be cleared through awareness and the changing of our old belief systems. This shift aligns us with our natural flow and the greater good.

The outside war is a reflection of the one we wage internally, where we fight ourselves to stay in control through our mind and the 'known' rather than **letting our heart resonance (unknown), lead the way and guide us into a whole new workable state of abundance where everybody prospers.**

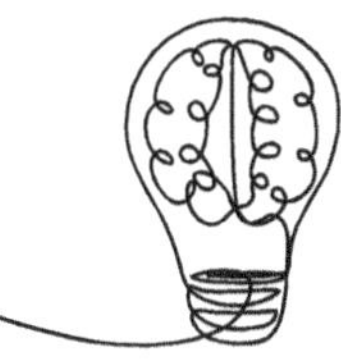

Gateway Eight – Creativity

Creativity helps open our abundance as it is life expressing itself through us. It's not something we do, it's energy we tap into and bring through to fruition. It's beyond the mind's control, where energy starts to move with an impulse, spark or sensation and finds its way to form, whether through words, color, sound, touch, taste or action.

It's the language of the soul, far deeper than intellect and flows from the same field that grows a forest, forms a heartbeat and turns a seed into a child. Creativity belongs to all, not just artists; it's a way of problem solving, telling stories, nurturing others, and birthing dreams.

When we create we open the door to the unknown where something new comes into existence and in that moment, we remember we are not separate from the endless stream of life itself. Creativity is not only about art or invention; it's about vision, curiosity, and the courage to bring forth something new.

It depends on our definition and perhaps a bigger picture description is influential – creators not only invented or imagined something new, but they also changed the way humanity saw itself. Think Buddha, Jesus, Lao Tzu, Socrates, Leonardo da Vinci, Albert Einstein, Nikola Tesla, Thomas Edison, Shakespeare, Michelangelo, Beethoven, Rumi, Gandhi, Amelia Earhart, Wangari Maathai, Marie Curie, Martin Luther

King Jr, Nelson Mandela, Maya Angelou and Mother Teresa to name a few.

The truth is, everyone is creative in some way, and it's not about fitting into a box, comparing results or fearing judgments, it's about expression! Some of the aforementioned creators continuously let their creativity flow through numbers, equations, testing, and the infinite posturing of ideas, until they finally, cracked the code.

It is the core of our deepest nature as human beings to create, to express, to bring the unseen into being. An idea may spark, however the true magic begins when our energy moves outwards and starts shaping into something to be shared.

When this expression is given to others they can feel the original source, whether through craft, words, sound, food, or performance, as it hits directly into the heart and awakens memory of the creativity residing in all of us.

We marvel at the creation of life itself, how a single sperm fertilizes a single egg and forms the first cell of a human being, developing into a newborn baby, the purest form of the unknown becoming known. Yet as a collective we've drifted away from this sacred creative knowing and prioritized the mind, the intellect, rules and measurable achievements, believing this is a better way to gain security, wealth and power. By doing this, we have undervalued creativity for the priceless natural gift it truly is.

Tune in to the last time you shed a tear. It was probably when you felt someone or something that touched your heart: a movie, a song, words, nature, whatever it was, you experienced your heart resonance reflecting back through a mirrored creation.

Even now as I write these words they arrive from nowhere known. It's a stream of thought flowing through to my fingertips, expressing itself into creation on the page. It comes through with purpose and expands my field of possibilities where more knowingness occurs and new information forms words.

Creativity delivers the greatest gift possible by reminding us we are all connected, all creators, and **all part of the same infinite source field, where every act of expression is a thread that weaves us back into the universal tapestry of life.**

Gateway Nine – Restoration of Orginal Love

What if we did come from this source field and didn't just arrive here by chance? What if, on a soul level, we chose our parents, not only to receive their love, but to help heal generational wounds and beliefs they couldn't? In doing so, we entered families with deep-rooted patterns, not to suffer under them, but to eventually awaken and rewrite them.

As a newborn we come into this incarnation carrying subtle imprints, strands from past lifetimes, ancestral patterns, and soul agreements made before birth. From the very first breath, beliefs begin to shape us, both those we arrive with, and others we absorb instantly from the world around us.

As we start to grow these influences affect us particularly if love is withdrawn or not available from parents. We automatically feel unlovable and unknowingly make decisions e.g. *Shut off and protect self* or *I'm going to hide my love to stay safe.*

Have you ever thought what was happening for your mother or your father when you were born? What were they going through emotionally, mentally, physically and spiritually?

We want our parents to be there for us and when they are unable, we unconsciously shut down our love and block them out because they have hurt us and we automatically feel unlovable, which translates to *our love is not enough*. This is where we need to heal our own wounds.

Disconnection from any original family member can padlock our love. The key to open it is often elusive and deeply buried beneath extreme sensitivity and hurt. Rejection is the bullseye for the painful arrow we've carried for lifetimes, and the shutdown point of our love.

While we can cope with physical separation from our original family, nobody copes well with spiritual separation, as it is not the truth. Even if there has been trauma and terrible behaviors, there is still a being with a heart that we are connected to by our original choice. Whoever is aware is the one who can move first by letting go, and opening their heart metaphysically – even if there is no physical contact, it frees our love.

It's from freedom our true nature flows, needing no protection, nor attack, as it is the source of our sovereignty and joins the missing links between our physical and spiritual connections into the oneness of love, from which we are born and return to.

This is why it is important to restore love in families as it relates to our purpose of being here. It's a personal awareness of the nature of our heart's resonance, which is constantly open. It's our mind's perception that supposedly closes it down. It's our ability to see the human 'being' beyond their negative behavior as we have all been conditioned, some more than others. We can't change anyone else and we can disagree with their behavior, however, when we reside in our true self, it's impossible to close our heart frequency to anyone.

Opening our heart
matters not whether
the person is physically
present, as this is an
energetic shift which
restores the generational
love-lines carried
through time and space.

...and it helps us
remember, we came
from love, we are love
and we return to love.

"We're all just walking each other home."

Ram Dass

Support

If you would like to experience more, here are the services Jilly provides to assist you on your travels.

All Wellbeing Programs promote personal and professional awareness growth and are undertaken with the willingness to look within.

Energy Matters Online Program (Download) – Travel through the 9 Transformational Gateways with Jilly's guidance. Available from **brightsparkhealth.com.au**

Personal Awareness Zoom Sessions – Gain deeper understanding and free yourself from limiting behaviors.

Relationship Sessions – Developing greater awareness to create authentic, loving relationships with self and others.

Conscious Leadership Mentoring Zoom Sessions – How to be a better leader by becoming more aware and creating teams that take self-responsibility.

Workplace Wellbeing Individual Zoom Program – Being able to confidentially release emotional upsets creates greater inner stability and resilience.

Workplace Wellbeing Team Zoom Program – Raising the awareness level of the group individually and as a collective to create better results.

Personal/Professional Group Workshops – Effective way for teams to improve their awareness of self and others by having real, heartfelt experiences together.

Staff Wellbeing Newsletters – Specifically created for businesses to address individual self-responsibility and promote common unity at work.

Contact

Websites
www.brightsparkhealth.com.au

Email
jilly@brightsparkhealth.com.au

Facebook
https://www.facebook.com/brightsparkhealth

Instagram
https:www.instagram.com/bright_spark_health

LinkedIn
linkedin https://www.linkedin.com/in/jilly-gabrielson-380560bb/

Monthly Wellbeing Newsletter
Sign Up: brightsparkhealth.com.au

About The Author

For more than 30 years, Jilly has worked as a wellbeing practitioner, counselor, facilitator, and writer, supporting thousands of individuals and organizations to break free from physical, mental, and emotional conditioning to reconnect with their true natural self. Her work blends professional expertise and tools with rare intuitive insight, supporting others to find their own answers by shining light on what was previously hidden and facilitating meaningful and lasting change.

Passionate about the universe, personal growth and expansive communication, Jilly continually shares her voice through personal and professional sessions, group work, corporate wellbeing programs, magazine articles, and emotional insight blogs which merge professional expertise with heartfelt love and human touch.

If you enjoyed reading my book I'd be most grateful for you to share a review on Amazon, Facebook, Instagram and of course with your family and friends who may benefit from reading Energy Matters!

Acknowledgments

Thank you to my wonderful family of origin, Mum, Dad, Raylee, Johnny and Gavin. To my ex-husband John, his sons Luke and Michael and my in-laws Greg, Jules and Heidi who have all supported my life at different times.

To my beautiful son Jack, daughter-in-law Ally and granddaughter Lily Claire, you light up my life with your never ending love and joy! Being a mother to you, Jack, has been the greatest gift of my life!

I also acknowledge my nephews, nieces and their families, as all have greatly contributed to my life in some way and are a constant in my heart.

To five very special friends who have walked beside me for the past twenty years, Helen, Trish, Yvette, Jules and Kathy. Thank you for your love, kindness, laughs and endless support. Also to many other friends who have been part of my life at various stages including Lisa, Lynette, Kerry, Helen, Dawn and Clint, I will always be grateful for your kindness and care.

To my clients over the years, thank you for finding me and so deeply adding to my life experiences and hopefully in some way, I've added to yours.

To my editor and friend Nic Karandonis for his belief, professional care and encouragement to keep me on track! Also to my Publisher Julie Postance, Editor Karen Crombie, Designer Sophie White and everyone who contributed to bringing this book to life!

To my spiritual family wherever you are and whether our paths have crossed or not, that familiar original tune of love has remained within for lifetimes and together we help each other to remember!

Lastly and very importantly, to you the reader, I'm so grateful to be harmonizing my note with yours as we play in the universal orchestra of life! ♪